I0616148

FELICIA CARTRIGHT

AND THE CASE OF THE
BLACK PHANTOM

Felicia   Joan

FELICIA CARTRIGHT

AND THE CASE OF THE
BLACK PHANTOM

BERNARD PALMER

ANEKO
PRESS

Felicia Cartright and the Case of the Black Phantom
© 2025 by Bernard Palmer
All rights reserved. First edition 1968.
Second edition 2025.

Please do not reproduce, store in a retrieval system, or transmit in
any form or by any means – electronic, mechanical, photocopying,
recording, or otherwise, without written permission from the publisher.

Scripture quotations from The Authorized (King James)
Version. Rights in the Authorized Version in the United
Kingdom are vested in the Crown. Reproduced by permission
of the Crown's patentee, Cambridge University Press.

Cover Artwork: Adobe Firefly & Ideogram

Editor: Charlene Miskimen

Aneko Press *Youth*

www.anekopress.com

Aneko Press, Life Sentence Publishing, and our logos are trademarks of
Life Sentence Publishing, Inc.
203 E. Birch Street
P.O. Box 652
Abbotsford, WI 54405

JUVENILE FICTION / Religious / Christian / Action & Adventure

Paperback ISBN: 979-8-88936-312-5

eBook ISBN: 979-8-88936-313-2

10 9 8 7 6 5 4 3 2 1

Available where books are sold

CONTENTS

CHAPTER 1

ARRIVAL

Felicia Cartright shifted her position slightly and leaned forward to peer out the window of the ranch pickup truck. Her attention was caught by the grotesquely beautiful jumble of rocks that made up the towering ridge to their right. Felicia and Joan Bailey, with their rancher-hostess at the wheel, had left Denver more than an hour before and were traveling straight west into the Rockies.

They had been to Colorado a number of times but never failed to be awed by the sheer granite cliffs reaching up for the sky or tumbling away to sickening depths below. Snow and fog shrouded the upper reaches of the hills above the timberline where naked rocks gleamed in the cold sun. At lower levels, aspen and evergreen covered the steep slopes where there was soil enough for them to dig in their fibrous roots and hang on. When the soil left, so did the vegetation, and, here and there, multicolored granite outcroppings contrasted with the green of the forest.

"I'd forgotten how beautiful it is out here," she exclaimed breathlessly.

For the moment, even Joan, whose chatter livened the entire third floor of the dorm at Wellington School for Girls, was silent – stilled by the quiet beauty of the scene around them.

"You'll never know how happy we were to get your invitation to come out and spend the summer with you," Felicia continued.

"That's right," Joan broke in. "After a whole year of Miss Duncan and the school, we're about ready for a rest. And especially me. I think Miss Duncan made a personal project of watching me all year."

A smile lighted Aunt Abigail Chandler's face. "Don't tell me you find Amelia difficult."

Joan gasped. Now she had done it! "Me and my big mouth! Now I'm in for it."

Abigail's laughter was warm and lilting.

"You and Miss Duncan are good friends, aren't you?" There was a tremor in Joan's voice.

"I don't suppose I have a better friend in all the world than Amelia Duncan. We've been friends since our own days at Wellington many years ago."

Joan's cheeks were crimson. "Are–are you going to tell her what I said?"

"Should I?"

"You can tell her that her problem child has gone and done it again."

Abigail tightened her grip on the wheel and expertly negotiated a hairpin curve. "I don't think that would serve any useful purpose, do you?"

Joan still did not entirely understand what Aunt Abigail was trying to tell her. "It would serve the purpose of causing more trouble with her than I've got already."

"I think we'll just forget that you said anything. How about that?"

Joan eyed her gratefully. "I'll be your slave forever."

The dude ranch owner was still chuckling a moment or two later.

"Don't tell anyone I ever said this," she began, "and especially Amelia. But there was a good reason why she was chosen to be the dean at Wellington. You see, when she was in school herself, she mastered all the tricks anybody had ever thought of and a lot they hadn't. When she got to be the dean, nobody could pull anything on her. She was onto every trick."

Joan's eyes sparkled. "So that accounts for that intuition all the girls say she has about what's going on in the dorm."

"Exactly." Abigail's smile took her back over her own years as a student at Wellington. "As a matter of fact, as I recall, she was something like you as a girl."

Joan stared. "You're kidding!"

Felicia found the comparison highly amusing.

She was still laughing when Aunt Abigail slowed the truck to make a left turn off the highway onto a narrow gravel road. For several minutes, nobody spoke.

"I'm glad to be able to tell you girls that the situation at the ranch is quite different than it was when you were here the last time. Now everything is going very well."

Joan glanced impishly at Felicia. "You mean we aren't going to have anybody to help? There won't be any mysteries to solve?"

"Nobody to help. No mysteries to solve," Mrs. Chandler repeated. "Does that make you feel bad?"

"Not me," Joan retorted. "Of course, Felicia might feel a little different. But if I know her, she'll find a little lamb without a mother or something."

Two spots of color showed in Felicia's cheeks.

They drove on in silence for thirty or forty minutes. Neither of them slept. They were much too excited for that, but they both had been tired when the trip west from Denver began. They allowed themselves only enough time to finish their exams at the Wellington School for Girls before catching the first plane from Boston to Denver. There Aunt Abigail met them, stopped only long enough to pick up an order of groceries, and headed for the ranch.

As they neared the ranch, Felicia's weariness fled. She looked around in something akin to wonder, remembering each hill and mountain stream.

"What's that brown area on the top of that ridge?" she asked after a time.

Aunt Abigail's smile faded. "There was a forest fire here this spring. I've never seen anything like it. The smoke hung over the valley until everything had an eerie reddish cast and the sun was the color of an orange. A lot of valuable timber was destroyed, and the bears and moose and elk came down into the pastures to get away from the fire. You would have thought our ranch was a national park for a while, there was so much game everywhere."

They talked about the fire for a time before lapsing into silence once more. They could see the ranch buildings ahead when Mrs. Chandler gave them another bit of information.

"I have a guest at the ranch I think I should tell you about."

Both girls eyed her quickly. There was a strange tone in her voice, as though the information she was giving was in the form of a warning.

"Of course, we have quite a number of guests this year, but Twyla is my husband's niece."

"I see," Felicia murmured.

"Twyla is–" She paused, searching for words. "She's – well, she's *different* than you girls are."

Joan and Felicia glanced at each other quickly but did not speak.

"I knew she was coming to spend some time with me this summer," Aunt Abigail went on, her mouth tightening to a straight, hard line. "But I didn't know she was going to be here at the same time as you two."

"That's perfectly all right." Felicia's smile was matched by Joan's.

"I was about to call and ask you to wait until later in the summer, but I got to thinking that you probably had your plans made, so I didn't."

"Don't worry about it," Joan assured her. "We'll like Twyla."

Aunt Abigail's head snapped around quickly. "I haven't told you everything. We've had some unexpected guests arrive and have been forced to do some reshuffling. I'm having to ask you girls to share a room with Twyla."

"That's all right too," Felicia said quickly. "We don't mind."

"I was sure you wouldn't." Her eyes snapped. "But Twyla feels that she has been highly insulted. She's been pouting around the place for the last three days."

Aunt Abigail pulled into the parking lot and stopped beside a sleek canary yellow sports car.

"Just leave your bags. I'll have one of the boys take them to your room."

There were a number of guests in the lounge as they went through – little groups of men and women wearing painfully new Western clothes and talking in cheery tones. Felicia looked for Twyla Chandler to see if she could pick her out before Aunt Abigail introduced them to her. But if she was in the room, the ranch owner didn't acknowledge her.

They stopped a time or two for Aunt Abigail to introduce them to some of the guests. By the time they got to their room, their suitcases were already there.

The room was large and airy, with three single beds and a large closet.

"It's beautiful!" Joan exclaimed.

"I'm glad you like it." Aunt Abigail moved in the direction of the door. "I'm sorry that I have to run. I'll introduce you to Twyla at dinner."

With that, she flew out of the room, and Felicia and Joan were alone.

"I'm curious," Felicia murmured as she closed the door, "about Twyla Chandler."

"It sounds as though she's going to be a lovely roommate," Joan said. She went over and opened the closet door. Twyla's clothes almost filled half of the large storage space. "I can see that already."

Felicia put her suitcase on the stand and opened it. While she removed her clothes and hung them in the closet, she talked to her friend.

"It sounds to me as though Twyla isn't exactly a favorite of Mrs. Chandler's."

"I got the same impression." Joan moved lazily across the room to her own suitcase. "I don't know why you have to be so efficient. Here we just get to the ranch, and I think I can take it easy for a few minutes. But what do you do? You start putting your clothes away and make me feel so ashamed of myself I've got to go to work too." She grinned. "When it comes to roommates, maybe Twyla will be an improvement."

"I was thinking the same thing."

The girls had just dressed for dinner when Aunt Abigail came for them.

"I want you to sit at my table this evening so I can catch up on all the news about Wellington." She had to leave them for a moment. "There's one more errand I have to attend to. I'll meet you in the dining room in a few minutes."

When they reached the dining room, it was almost filled. Some of the guests were already eating.

"I don't see Aunt Abigail," Joan said, "do you?"

Felicia nodded. "Right over there."

The older woman was standing near a small table talking with a tall, slender, handsome young man. He was six feet tall and bronzed with sandy hair.

"Say, now," Joan muttered in a hoarse whisper. "That guy looks interesting."

"Miss Bailey," Felicia said, mimicking Miss Duncan's austere manner, "you know that a Wellington girl does not take up with strange young men. They must be properly introduced by a person of integrity who knows them both over an acceptable period of time."

Joan made a little face at her. "Who's talking about taking up with anybody? I just said he looks interesting."

Felicia laughed. "I know what you said." By this time, they were within a few feet of the table.

Mrs. Chandler saw them and turned abruptly. "Oh, there you are. I've been looking for you." She turned back to the young man. "You'll have to excuse me," she said. "I have guests I must entertain."

"Certainly." However, he did not move. "I don't believe I've met your guests, Mrs. Chandler."

There was nothing for her to do except introduce him.

"This," she said, her voice sounding very much like Miss Duncan's when she was echoing disapproval, "is Mr. Sherman."

"Now, Aunt Abigail," he said, his voice light and bantering. "You know as well as I do that my first name is John."

The corners of her mouth drooped, and the lines across her forehead deepened.

"And these girls are from my old alma mater back in Boston, Wellington School for Girls."

"Now that sounds interesting." He noticed that there was an extra plate at the table. "May I join you?"

The girls glanced at Aunt Abigail.

"I suppose it would be all right," she said without enthusiasm.

He helped them get seated and took the chair between Joan and Felicia.

"You know," he began, "I've been trying to do

business with Mrs. Chandler for the last two or three days, but she doesn't even have time to listen to me."

The older woman straightened primly. "I've already told you that I don't have what you're after, John. And I am very busy."

His dark eyes were fixed on Felicia. "Maybe you girls can talk some sense into her head."

Before anyone could speak, Aunt Abigail was called away. Almost immediately, a slender, willowy brunette entered the dining room. She moved a step or two inside the door and paused, as though she were looking for someone. She was about the same age as Felicia and Joan, but there was an air of sophistication about her. She was strikingly dressed, and her hair was done beautifully.

Eyes turned in her direction as she came into the dining room. Although she tried to act as though it didn't matter to her, it was apparent that she enjoyed the attention. She remained motionless for a brief moment, and then spying John Sherman, she glided in his direction.

"Hello, John." A faint smile teased her lips.

He looked up. "Hi."

"I've been looking all over for you."

He colored slightly. "I had some things to do today."

"Oh, you're always busy," she said, pouting. "Come on, I've been saving a table for the two of us."

He was obviously embarrassed. "I'm sorry, but I've got some business with your aunt."

Twyla stared frostily at Joan and Felicia. "So I see." He could avoid introducing her to them no longer.

"We're glad to know you, Twyla," Felicia said, trying hard to be friendly.

The muscles in the girl's face tightened. "I suppose you're the girls I am having to share my room with?" Ice filmed her words. "I suppose you're from that school she used to go to."

"And it's a fine school," the young man broke in. "One of the finest finishing schools in the East."

"Really, John?" she exclaimed. "I didn't know you were an authority on girls' finishing schools."

He laughed carelessly. "You'd be surprised at what I'm an authority on."

Her eyes flashed. Felicia could see that she was used to having her own way.

"If you aren't going to join me, I'll find someone else."

"I'm sorry, Twyla." But he didn't sound sorry at all. "I'll see you tomorrow."

"If I'm not too busy." She flounced away.

The trio at the table watched until she sat down at the opposite end of the dining room.

"So," Sherman murmured, "you should be properly awed. You have just met Twyla the Great."

Although there was a lively, bantering tone in his voice, his face grew serious as he looked around the room. He, too, seemed to be looking for someone – apprehensively. Satisfied that whomever he was looking for was not in the dining room at the moment, he directed his attention to Felicia and Joan once more.

"You know," he said guardedly, just above a whisper, "I wasn't kidding a few minutes ago when I said that I'd like to have you talk some sense into Abigail Chandler's head."

The girls both eyed him curiously.

"What do you mean?" Felicia asked.

He seemed disturbed and secretive. "You won't tell her that I talked with you, will you?" he asked.

"Not unless she asks us about it," Joan told him.

His smile creased the corners of his mouth. "You mean you wouldn't lie a little for me?"

She shook her head. "No," she went on, "I wouldn't lie for you, and neither would Felicia."

"But," Felicia added, "unless Aunt Abigail asks us a direct question that we have to answer, we won't say anything to her."

He shrugged indifferently. "Maybe I ought to talk to Twyla. I'm sure a little falsehood or two wouldn't bother her any." He paused, then spoke again. "I guess it won't make much difference if you tell Abigail I talked with you or not. I don't think it'll budge her any."

Joan leaned forward curiously. "Now you have got me wondering what this is all about."

"I work for a wealthy polo enthusiast in the East," he said. "He sent me out here to buy a certain stallion from Mrs. Chandler, but she claims she doesn't have him."

Felicia could not remain silent. "I'm sure that if Aunt Abigail told you she doesn't have this horse, she doesn't have him."

Mr. Sherman frowned.

"I might have known you'd be sticking up for her. From what I've heard about Wellington, all the girls stick together." Before either Joan or Felicia could reply, he continued. "She tells me that she's only training polo ponies. She doesn't have any breeding stock. But my employer says she owns this stallion, and he wants him." He paused, breathing deeply. "And my employer is an extremely wealthy man. He usually gets what he wants."

He lowered his voice.

"So if you girls would help me, I'd sure appreciate it. All I want you to do is convince her that she ought to let us buy this animal. We'll pay her well for him."

"We can tell her," Felicia answered, "but Aunt Abigail is a Christian. She wouldn't lie to you."

He stared at her.

"Well, do what you can. It's my job if I go back without that horse. Just remember that!"

CHAPTER 2

COMPLICATIONS

After a moment or two, John Sherman got to his feet. "I just remembered something," he said apologetically. "Something that I've got to talk to Twyla about. Will you excuse me, please?"

With that, he was gone. "Now we know where we stand," Felicia said, laughing quietly. "About three notches below Twyla Chandler."

"Look over there," Joan said with some amusement. "Twyla doesn't seem to be very angry with him for sitting with us."

Aunt Abigail came back. "Where's John?" she asked.

"He just remembered something he had to talk to Twyla about."

"That girl!" Abigail sighed. "I'm afraid she throws herself at him shamefully."

"And now our hearts are broken," Joan reminded her.

Aunt Abigail stiffened the same way Miss Duncan did when she was about to deliver one of her famous lectures on studying or the conduct of Wellington girls.

"I'm sure either of you could do better than John Sherman."

Joan glanced at her obliquely. "From the way he talked to us, he seems to prefer older women." There was no mistaking Joan's chiding implication.

Mrs. Chandler snorted indignantly. "What he really wants is something I haven't got and never even had," she exclaimed, pulling in a deep breath. "Somehow John got it into his head that we have a valuable stallion on the ranch. He keeps following me around telling me that his employer wants to buy the horse and insisting that I put a price on him."

"That's strange, isn't it?"

"It's more than strange." Her lips clipped the words. "It's disgusting. If I owned an animal like the one he's talking about, I'd be eager to sell him, but I don't. We haven't had a stallion on the ranch for years. I've tried to tell him that, but he won't believe me."

Now that Aunt Abigail had started to talk about the reason for John's appearance at the ranch, it was easy for them to draw her out on the subject.

"Mr. Sherman must have some reason for being so insistent," Felicia observed quietly. "Have you ever asked him why he thinks you have the horse when you don't?"

"All he says is that he knows I've got him, and his

employer wants him. But I–" The words caught in her throat in midsentence. Her eyes gleamed.

Both girls saw the change that came flashing over her.

"What is it?" Joan asked.

But Aunt Abigail wasn't listening. "No," she said scarcely above a whisper. "It couldn't be – It couldn't be."

By this time, Joan and Felicia were staring at her. Surely Aunt Abigail would remember if she owned a valuable stallion. That would be like forgetting an expensive automobile or a five-karat diamond ring. Yet that look in her eyes told them she had just remembered something.

"What is it?" Felicia insisted. "Did you remember you do own the horse after all?"

"Of course not." Aunt Abigail's indignation flashed. "I'm not so old I'd forget a thing like that. But–" Her voice grew thoughtful. "But I do remember something about a stallion. Only it happened before my husband died." The corners of her mouth firmed, and her body stiffened. "It couldn't have anything to do with this."

The girls waited. It was a few moments before the older woman continued.

"For several years, my husband had dreamed of raising polo ponies," she finally went on. "He thought he could develop a hardy strain that would be able to stand the rigors of polo better than Eastern-raised ponies. And he had some ideas about training them that he felt would be an improvement. That was going to be a major project for the ranch, but he became sick not long after that and was never able to finish his plans."

"That was too bad," Felicia murmured.

"Yes, it was one of the reasons we were in such financial difficulties at the time of his death. He had bought this expensive stallion colt and–"

Felicia and Joan glanced quickly at each other.

"Maybe that's the one John Sherman has been talking about."

"It couldn't be," Abigail retorted quickly. "That animal has been dead for five years."

Felicia toyed with her fork. Aunt Abigail had only told them part of the story.

After a time, she continued.

"When my husband decided to do something, he always wanted to do it better than anyone else. It was the same with this matter of raising polo ponies. He found the best stallion colt in this part of the country and borrowed the money to buy him." Her smile brightened. "He was the most beautiful little animal we ever had on the ranch."

Aunt Abigail paused to speak to a guest going by.

"We hadn't had Nugget more than a few weeks," she went on, "when he got distemper and almost died. It was during the winter and the roads were blocked, so we couldn't get the vet to come out, so I nursed him back to health." Her smile returned. "Nugget was fiery and almost unmanageable, except for me. He seemed to remember that I had befriended him, and whenever I went to the corral, he'd come over to me. I could put a halter on him or take hold of his mane and lead him anywhere."

"And you say he died?"

Mrs. Chandler nodded. "Actually, he was killed. One of our hands was taking him to a neighboring ranch when he was two years old. The trailer hitch broke on a mountain curve, and the trailer and horse both went over the cliff."

Felicia gasped. For an instant or two, Aunt Abigail's eyes clouded as she remembered.

"Nugget was killed and buried at the bottom of the cliff."

"That is too bad," Joan murmured.

Abigail nodded. "We both cried as we stood beside the place where Joe buried him."

The waitress had brought their dinners, but the plates sat forgotten before them getting cold.

"My husband was already quite ill at the time," she went on. "I always have felt that the loss of Nugget might have hastened his death."

The girls nodded, as though to agree with her.

"Do you suppose John thinks you still have Nugget and won't tell him?"

Mrs. Chandler shrugged. "I don't know, and I don't care."

With that, she changed the subject quickly.

Felicia and Joan didn't realize how tired they were until they got to their room later in the evening. Then they realized that their bodies were drained of strength.

"Think we ought to wait up for Twyla?"

Joan shook her head. "It may be the middle of the night before she gets in, and I'm exhausted."

Felicia kicked off her shoes. "I feel sorry for Twyla, somehow. She tries so hard to be sophisticated. She doesn't know that real happiness doesn't come from that direction."

"No," Joan retorted, "but she certainly thinks it does."

They had finished their evening devotions and were in bed when Felicia spoke about Twyla again.

"Do you suppose she knows that Jesus died for her sins, Joan? Do you suppose she's ever been challenged with the claims Christ has on her life?"

"Knowing Aunt Abigail, I'm sure she has."

Felicia turned on her side and rose on her elbow. "I just remembered. We didn't pray for her."

The girls stirred in their sleep as Twyla came in sometime after one in the morning, but she turned the light off quickly, and they drifted back to sleep. The following morning, she was still asleep when they got up. The girls hurried to the dining room for breakfast. John had arrived ahead of them and was seated across the room.

"Well, are you going to talk to our young man?" Joan asked, eyes dancing.

"You can talk to him if you want to."

"Oh, no," Joan replied quickly. "Never let it be said that I stepped in ahead of my very best friend."

"Be my guest."

At that moment, John spied them and hurried across the dining room. "There you are. I was afraid I had missed you."

He pulled out chairs for them and sat down himself. "Well," he said eagerly, "did you get to talk to Abigail?"

Felicia nodded.

"What did she say?"

"The same thing she said to you."

Disappointment dulled his handsome young face. "Don't tell me she gave that same old story again."

"She still claims there isn't a stallion on the ranch if that's what you mean."

They were just finishing breakfast when Twyla came in. Her entrance was a repeat of that she made the previous night. She was wearing a pair of jeans and a Western shirt, open at the throat. She held her white Stetson hat carelessly at her side, as though she had picked it up as an afterthought. In spite of her casual clothes, one would have thought she stepped from the cover of an exclusive fashion magazine.

She saw John sitting with Felicia and Joan, but she did not start in their direction immediately. Instead, she surveyed the dining room as though looking for someone much more important and then began to saunter among the tables. The girls both saw her and knew where she was headed even though her route was devious. At last, she reached the table and stood quite still.

"Well, I see you Wellington girls are getting acquainted."

Joan grinned impishly. "Yes, we're doing quite well, thank you."

Twyla was smiling, but daggers glinted in her dark eyes. "May I join you?" she asked. "Or is this a private party?"

"There's nothing private about breakfast," John said indifferently. "I was about to tell the girls that my job here is finished. I've decided to go back East."

Twyla recoiled as though he had slapped her suddenly. "You're going back so soon?" The hurt in her voice was deep. "I–I thought you were going to stay here for another two weeks."

He grinned. "That's what I had planned, but I've had to make some changes." He finished the last of his coffee and stood. "I'm sorry, I'll see you around."

For an instant or two after he left, Felicia was afraid that Twyla was going to cry. Her eyes became luminous, and her thin, pale lips trembled slightly.

At last, she looked defiantly from Felicia to Joan. "I'm sure you realize that John and I are good friends," she informed them. "As a matter of fact, we're very good friends."

Felicia read the concern in her voice. "Joan and I were just visiting with him," she explained. "We aren't interested in dating him."

That seemed to afford Twyla a measure of relief, but she was determined not to show it. "That means nothing to me one way or the other," she said archly.

Aunt Abigail came into the dining room just then and sat down at their table. She tried to smile, but it didn't come off very well. Consternation was stamped on her usually pleasant features.

The girls saw it immediately.

"Is there something wrong?" Joan asked.

Aunt Abigail moistened her lips with the tip of her tongue. She hesitated, as though uncertain whether to speak or not.

"What is it?" Felicia urged.

"Nothing that you would be able to do anything about."

"Now you do have us curious," Twyla put in.

Mrs. Chandler laughed.

"Now I suppose I will have to tell you in order to keep you from worrying. My foreman, Pete Weaver, was in a few minutes ago – you remember I told you that we've been taking some polo ponies to train?"

The girls nodded.

"Well," she said, "two expensive mares that belong to other people have been stolen!"

"Are you sure?"

"Pete says that they could have strayed away and broken the fence, but he doesn't think so."

"That is too bad," Felicia murmured.

"The mares were insured so there isn't any financial loss, but it could ruin our plans for building a reputation as the trainers of polo ponies." She breathed deeply. "And just when I thought all of our problems were ironed out."

CHAPTER 3

TWYLA'S PROBLEM

Felicia was so disturbed it seemed to her that conversation in the entire dining room had ceased and everyone was staring at their table. Aunt Abigail Chandler did have trouble, after all. Only this time, it was something they couldn't help.

"What makes Pete think the horses were stolen?" Twyla asked. "He must have a reason."

Aunt Abigail nodded. "He has got a reason. Several of them. The fence is in excellent condition for one thing. Pete has been our foreman for years and has always had the reputation for maintaining the best fences in the county. So he doesn't see how those mares could have broken out."

Twyla shrugged. "Sounds like pride to me. He just doesn't want to admit he did a miserable job on the fence. You'll probably find a number of broken places if you send someone out to ride fence."

"If we do, it would be the first time."

Silence crackled tensely between them.

"What were the other reasons Mr. Weaver had for thinking the horses were stolen?" Joan asked.

"They were well broken," she said, "and far enough into the training so they were not difficult to control."

She paused.

"What other reasons did he have?" Twyla persisted.

Aunt Abigail stood abruptly, ending the conversation.

"Pete had reasons enough to make him believe the horses were stolen," she announced, "and I have confidence enough in his judgment to go along with it."

Even Twyla did not dare to contradict her when her eyes flashed as they were flashing now.

"Of course," she went on, "that doesn't mean Pete is ruling out the fact that the horses may have broken the fence and wandered away. He's putting a man to riding fence and several others to riding the breaks in an effort to locate them."

Then, as though she couldn't stay angry more than a moment or two, her face softened. "Pete asked me to ride out with him to take a look around," she said. "Would you girls like to join me?"

Excitement flickered in Felicia's eyes. "Oh, we'd love to!"

Joan groaned under her breath. "Here we go again," she muttered.

Mrs. Chandler turned to her quizzically. "Pardon me?"

"I just made a silly remark," she countered. "It was nothing."

"Why don't you get into more comfortable clothes for riding and meet me at the barn in a few minutes?"

They started away, but Felicia turned back. "Would you like to go with us, Twyla?"

"I think not." Her voice was sulky and petulant. "I have other things to do."

The girls changed quickly and left their room. They were just going outside when they met Aunt Abigail with Twyla in tow.

"Oh, there you are," she exclaimed, rushing over to them. "I completely forgot that I won't be able to go with you this morning. I have to go into Denver to pick up some new guests who are flying in." She stopped momentarily. "Were you going to ride anyway?"

Felicia started to say they weren't, but something in the older woman's eyes caused her to change her mind.

"We hadn't really talked about it, but I think it would be nice, don't you, Joan?"

Aunt Abigail did not wait for Joan's reply. "That's fine." She turned to Twyla. "You can go riding with the girls this morning."

Twyla did not reply immediately, but the corners

of her mouth drew into an insolent pout. "I suppose it's better than nothing."

Joan would have retorted hotly, but she stopped, reminding herself that she was a Christian and didn't do such things.

They went to the barn and told the wrangler they wanted saddle horses. He got their mounts ready and led them out into the brilliant mountain sunshine.

"You aren't going far, are you?" he asked.

Twyla's temper flared. "We're perfectly capable of taking care of ourselves," she snapped, swinging expertly into the saddle.

The wrangler eyed her with bland amusement.

"I'm well aware of that, miss. Unfortunately, however, we have to go out and hunt for some of these folks who are perfectly capable of taking care of themselves. And it's not much fun for anybody."

"Well, you've never had to hunt for me, have you?" A superior little smile began to play with the corners of her mouth. "Of course, I don't know about Felicia and Joan. I'm not sure whether they can take care of themselves or not."

"Neither are we," Joan broke in quickly. "And I'm not eager to spend all night lost on some mountain slope." She told the wrangler where they were going and how long they would be gone.

They rode out across the west pasture where the polo ponies had been kept.

"I get so mad at these cowhands!" Twyla exploded.

"I was born here on the ranch, and I know horses and these hills better than they do, but they treat me as though I'm stupid."

Felicia shifted position in the saddle. "You were born here?"

Twyla nodded. "My dad was in partnership with Uncle Carl and Aunt Abigail until I was ten years old. Then Uncle Carl and Aunt Abigail got this stupid religion."

Felicia and Joan glanced quickly at one another. Twyla revealed her contempt for the things of God by the tone of her voice.

"Don't you even go to church?" Joan asked.

Twyla reined up and stared at her incredulously. "Do you?"

"Of course, we do," Felicia said. "At least, we go when we have the chance."

"Dad always said that Aunt Abigail and Uncle Carl had enough religion for everybody in the family."

They were riding across the rough west pasture as they talked.

"Of course, that can't be," Felicia told her seriously. "Nobody can have faith enough to save anyone else. Each one of us is going to have to give account to God for the sin in our lives. And if we haven't put our trust in Jesus Christ to save us, we're lost."

Twyla's eyes grew round. "You sound just like Aunt Abigail," she said lamely. With that, she lapsed into silence for a time. "Dad always said that if he hadn't sold out and gotten away from them, they'd have had him eating out of the same bowl of soup. I know now what he meant."

They rode on in silence.

"I wonder if they will find those horses," Joan said.

"I'm sure I wouldn't know," Twyla retorted, sneering. "I'm not particularly interested in Aunt Abigail's horses."

However, Felicia disagreed with her. "I'm curious to know what happened to them. They seem to have vanished so mysteriously."

"I still wonder if they didn't stray," Joan said. "They could have broken through the fence and gotten up into the hills. And if that happened, it might take weeks to find them."

Felicia nodded. "It does sound logical – if they broke out." She stood in the stirrups and surveyed the vast reaches of grass and timber around them. If the horses broke out, there would be a break in the fence where they went through. It should be an easy thing to prove one way or the other.

Twyla spoke up sharply, changing the subject. "I don't know about you, but I've got to get back. John and I were going out this afternoon."

Felicia turned to Joan. They hadn't planned on going back until the middle of the afternoon. They had some sandwiches the cook fixed for them in their saddle bags. But they actually weren't solving anything by–

Felicia straightened in the saddle.

"What's the matter with you?" Joan asked.

"Look over there!" Her finger wavered as she pointed toward the rocky hill a couple of hundred yards ahead.

"I don't see anything."

"I don't either," Twyla retorted impatiently.

"What are you trying to do? Scare us?"

"I–I–" Her voice was trembling so much she stopped and began again. "I saw a man hiding behind the rocks watching us!"

For an instant, fear gleamed in Twyla's dark eyes. She acted as though she was about to turn and go dashing back to the ranch at top speed.

"I–I'm sure it's just a hunter," Joan said hopefully. "Or–"

"They don't allow hunting this time of year," Twyla informed her.

"Or maybe it's a camper or–"

"Or a horse thief!" Felicia added.

"You would have to bring that up!" Joan exclaimed.

The girls looked at one another uncertainly.

"What do you think we ought to do?" Felicia asked at last.

Joan was staring beyond her and Twyla at the rocks where her friend saw the man watching them – or thought she had.

"I don't know about you," she retorted, "but I

think I've had enough horseback riding for today. I'm going back to the ranch."

Felicia looked up at the rocks again curiously.

"I sure would like to know what that guy was watching us for," she said.

"Well," Twyla told her, "if you want to find out, you're going to have to do it without me. I've got a previous engagement."

"So have I," Joan broke in. "As of right now."

Felicia laid the reins on her horse's neck to turn him around.

"I guess we might just as well go, but I would like to know why that man was spying on us."

Aunt Abigail had left for Denver when they got back to the ranch, and it was the middle of the afternoon before she returned. Felicia and Joan called her aside as soon as possible and told her what had happened.

"Are you sure the man was spying on you?" Mrs. Chandler wanted to know. "There are quite a lot of people around the ranch this time of year. It could have been someone who was on a very honest and legitimate errand."

"I suppose that could be," Joan answered, "but I sure didn't want to stick around to find out."

"I'm glad you came back rather than riding on under circumstances like that," Aunt Abigail said, "but I do feel that there must be some logical explanation for what happened."

When the girls went to their room sometime

later, Twyla was lying on her bed, her face buried in the pillow.

"Twyla!" Felicia exclaimed, hurrying over to her. "What's wrong?"

For a moment or two, she said nothing. Felicia put a hand on her shoulder. "What happened?" she asked gently.

Twyla stopped crying and sat up, wiping at her eyes.

"I–I saw John after we had breakfast this morning, and he said he was going to wait a day or two before leaving. But he didn't. He went off as soon as we rode away and–and he didn't even say goodbye."

She started to sob again quietly.

"He'll probably be getting in touch with you in a few days," Felicia said. "He seemed to like you a great deal."

Twyla looked up pathetically. In an instant, all of her sophistication seemed to melt away. She seemed actually younger than either Felicia or Joan.

"Do you really think so?"

Felicia nodded, smiling. "Now why don't you go with us down to the kitchen. We'll see if we can talk the cook out of some coffee or a glass of milk."

Twyla hesitated. "I–I don't think I can face anybody after–after what happened."

"Nothing happened," Joan said. "As far as anyone else is concerned, John finished what he was doing here and went home. There's nothing unusual about that."

Twyla looked from Felicia to Joan and back again. "Are–are you going to tell anyone?"

"We won't even mention it to Aunt Abigail," Felicia assured her.

Twyla went in, washed her face in cold water, and brushed her hair. In a moment, she had removed all but the faintest trace of her crying spell. They went down to the kitchen, and the cook gave them some coffee and rolls. The three of them sat there talking as though nothing had happened to upset Twyla. By the time they were ready to leave, she was feeling much better.

"I can never thank you enough," she murmured.

"You don't have to thank us," Joan said. "We get to feeling down once in a while ourselves. Maybe you'll have a chance to cheer us up."

"I've never had friends like you two before."

As they went out of the kitchen, the front door opened, and Twyla stopped suddenly, staring. "John!" she cried.

"Well, now," he said, "I didn't think I had been gone that long."

"But–but you told us that you were going back East." Her smile flickered briefly on her lips.

"A woman isn't the only one who has the right to change her mind." His smile was infectious. "Actually, I got a foolish notion that I was going to leave, so I checked out and drove to town. Then I got to thinking that I still had some more vacation time. So I came back to spend it."

Twyla smiled brightly. She looked at Felicia and Joan and winked.

"And where is that charming hostess? I've got to tell her that I want my room back before she puts somebody else in it."

"Come on," Twyla said, taking his arm, "let's go find her."

CHAPTER 4

PUZZLEMENT

The following morning, Felicia and Joan rode out to the west pasture with Pete Weaver and Aunt Abigail.

"I'm glad you were able to come out here with me this morning, Mrs. Chandler," the ranch foreman said. "I want to show you what I think happened to those mares."

"You don't have to do that, Pete." Her smile flashed. "You know that I've got the utmost confidence in you and your judgment."

"I wish I could say the same for myself." He shook his head in bewilderment. "There are some things about this affair that I can make out, but there are others that have got me fooled."

He took them to a spot near the ranch buildings and reined up.

"Now as nearly as the boys and I can determine,

the horses were grazing in this part of the pasture. The tracks were comparatively fresh yesterday morning." He pointed to the bare ground of an old roadbed that was liberally sprinkled with tracks. "Then somebody drove them in this direction."

"That seems quite obvious," Aunt Abigail acknowledged.

"That's what we thought when we got this far. But this is the part that was easy to figure out."

They were able to follow the tracks far enough to get the general direction the horses had been taken. Then they lost them on the hard clay bordering the creek.

"We had an awful time figuring out what happened next," Pete said. "If those thieves hadn't been running the horses so hard, we'd never have found any more tracks. But as it was, they drove them across the creek, and we picked up some deep hoofprints there."

Aunt Abigail nodded.

"And there was some bare ground near the fence that showed the same hoofprints. So we concluded that the horses were taken in this direction to the pasture fence."

The rancher did not reply. What her foreman said seemed simple enough to her, and it was all very logical. She couldn't quite understand what disturbed him so much. Somebody had rounded up the horses and drove them to the fence where they cut the wire and took them through. They probably had a big truck parked in the hills somewhere to get them out of the country as fast as possible. But she did not voice her opinion to Pete Weaver.

Pete guided them to the fence and dismounted.

"Now this is what stumps me, Mrs. Chandler," he said. "See these tracks?"

"Of course."

"Take a look at 'em. A good long look."

"I have," she retorted irritably.

"See anything strange about them?"

She shook her head.

"Those mares jumped that fence. Every last one of 'em!"

She jerked upright to stare at him.

"Are you sure?"

"I'd stake my life on it."

"But how could anyone do that?" she demanded. "And why?"

"That's what I can't figure out. How do you make horses you're driving jump a fence? Any horses I've ever seen have turned when they come to wire."

Abigail was thoughtful.

"And besides, it's so useless," she said. "It would only take half a minute with a pair of wire cutters to make a hole in a fence. Why would the thieves make such valuable horses jump, even if they could, and take a chance of getting them cut up in the wire?"

Pete pushed his battered old hat on the back of his head and scratched his ear with his forefinger.

"See what I mean about this being strange. I don't mind telling you, it's got me beat."

Felicia leaned forward to stare curiously at the deep hoofprints. There had to be some simple, logical explanation for all of this, but what was it?

"Have you tried to follow the tracks on the other side of the fence, Pete?" Aunt Abigail asked at last.

"The boys and I did manage to follow them for a couple of miles before we lost them. And that's another thing. You'd think the thieves would have slowed down once they got the horses out of the pasture, but not the guys who stole these mares. They were running as hard a mile and a half from here as they were when they cleared this fence."

The foreman talked with Aunt Abigail about the advisability of contacting the county sheriff. They decided on doing so when Pete got back that evening.

"I hate to go to the sheriff with the kind of story we've got right now," he said. "He'll think we're all crazy."

"He should be notified," she said, "regardless of the sort of evidence we have for him."

"I know that," he retorted curtly, "but we've got to have something to tell him. These horses can run off by themselves. And I think the sheriff would take a dim view of my running in to him with a story of a theft when we hadn't made an effort to see if they have strayed."

"But you said yourself that you're sure they've been stolen," Joan put in.

"My knowing that and the sheriff knowing it are two different things." He glanced at his watch. "I'm going to check with the boys who came out about sunup this morning to see if they've found anything. If they haven't, I'll call Sam Getty." He glanced in Aunt Abigail's direction. "If you're through with me, Mrs. Chandler, I'll be going."

"Go right ahead, Pete. We'll make our way back all right."

With that, he turned abruptly and rode away. The girls and Aunt Abigail remained where they were.

"This is getting more mysterious all the time," Joan said, more to herself than to Felicia or Mrs. Chandler.

Felicia lifted the reins as though to start the ride back to the house but stopped and turned in the saddle to face her companions. "You don't suppose John had anything to do with this, do you?" she asked.

Aunt Abigail's eyes narrowed. "What makes you ask that?"

"I don't know for sure." She laughed uneasily. "Now that I think of it, it sounds sort of silly, but he is interested in horses. Or at least he says he is. It seems like quite a coincidence to me."

The ranch owner's eyes narrowed thoughtfully. "It's strange that you would say that, Felicia. I've had some serious doubts about him myself. And especially after last night when he came back after checking out and giving me a forwarding address for his mail."

"He told us that he changed his mind and decided to spend the rest of his vacation here," Joan said.

"We thought perhaps he did it because he wanted to spend some more time with Twyla."

"With Twyla?" Aunt Abigail exclaimed. "Piffle! He doesn't care anything about going out with her. I've tried to tell her that, but she won't listen."

"Of course, there isn't any law against a person changing his mind," Joan reminded them. "If there were, I'd be in real trouble."

Mrs. Chandler turned her horse and clucked to him to begin the ride back to the ranch house.

"I've been trying to decide whether to tell you what happened last night," she said, "that added to my concern about John."

Felicia misunderstood her hesitation. "You don't have to tell us if you'd rather not."

"It isn't that." Aunt Abigail laughed nervously. "I was just trying to decide whether you'd think I'm a silly old woman if I tell you the other thing that happened that increased my doubts about Mr. Sherman."

"Don't let that bother you," Joan broke in. "You ought to hear some of the crazy ideas Felicia comes out with sometimes, and I haven't had her locked up yet."

Aunt Abigail formed her words with care. "Last night, John spent a long time visiting with me. He didn't keep asking me about this nonexistent stallion he wants to buy. Instead, he wanted to know if I did my own bookkeeping and if I managed the ranch and our summer guest business as well."

"I can understand his interest in that," Felicia said. "I've had several people marvel that you're able to keep everything going the way you do."

"But that isn't the sort of thing that interested him. He was asking if I had my office here in the house and if I had a safe to keep my money in and that sort of thing – the kind of questions most people won't put into words even if they do wonder about them."

"That is strange," the girls admitted.

"And that's not all. This morning before breakfast, I heard somebody in the living area of the house. I thought perhaps it was one of the new guests who had wandered into the wrong room. But when I went in, there was John."

Joan gasped. "In your apartment?"

"In my apartment and not ten feet from the door to my office."

"I don't blame you for being concerned," Felicia said. "He wouldn't have any legitimate reason for going into the part of the house where you live."

"That's exactly the thought that struck me," Aunt Abigail went on.

Aunt Abigail would have continued, but there was a sudden rattle in the grass to her right. Her horse reared and screamed in terror.

She fell to the ground!

Abigail Chandler's horse started to bolt, but the instant the reins came down, he stopped obediently. The muscles in his shoulders were quivering, and his nostrils flared in terror. But Felicia and Joan didn't notice the horse. They leaped off their own mounts and dashed to Aunt Abigail's side.

"Aunt Abigail!" Felicia cried. "Are you hurt?"

CHAPTER 5

RIDING ACCIDENT

The woman on the ground clenched her teeth against the pain and fought the nausea that swept over her.

"Aunt Abigail!" Felicia shouted.

"I–I–" She groaned involuntarily, closing her eyes. "I think it's my hip."

By this time, Felicia and Joan had regained control of themselves. Their eyes met questioningly.

"What're we going to do?" Joan asked, scarcely mouthing the words.

"We can't move her. That's for sure. Why don't you ride back to the ranch for help? I'll stay here."

Joan mounted her horse and rode away at top speed. The wiry cow pony seemed to know the importance of speed. He stretched out along the ground, straining every fiber of his being. Joan leaned forward, clenching the saddle with her knees. At first, fear gripped her, but as they flew over the rough ground, she began to regain her confidence. Before they had gone half a mile, she was whispering in her horse's ear, urging him to even greater speed.

Felicia made Aunt Abigail as comfortable as possible. For a time, the older woman lay back, closing her eyes. Sweat stood out on her forehead, and her arms were trembling convulsively. It was several minutes before the pain eased so she could speak.

"I–I don't know what was the matter with me," she muttered, scolding herself. "I know better than to sit a horse so loosely, especially out here where there're apt to be rattlesnakes to spook them."

"Don't try to talk," Felicia told her. "Joan will be back with help in a little while."

Mrs. Chandler winced. "I can't have this," she protested. "I'm much too busy to be laid up." She winced as the pain came surging back.

Felicia wiped the perspiration from her forehead and began to pray. It was almost an hour before the ranch vehicle came careening into view. Aunt Abigail heard them and opened her eyes.

"They're here," Felicia told her.

The injured woman sighed her relief.

A moment later, the vehicle lurched to a stop, and Joan and John got out.

"How is she?" Joan exclaimed.

"Ashamed of myself," Mrs. Chandler managed. "A woman my age ought to know better than to pull a crazy stunt like this. Especially when I've got so terribly much to do."

John took charge. "I improvised a stretcher for you, Mrs. Chandler," he said. "We'll have to be careful not to move that hip of yours while we're putting you in the truck."

Aunt Abigail tried to move.

"If you help me, I think I can get up and get into the truck myself."

"Oh, no, you don't," Felicia said firmly. "We're not going to take a chance on hurting you any worse than you're hurt already."

"That's right," John said. "And we've got to hurry. You need medical attention."

With the help of the girls, he was able to get Aunt Abigail into the back of the truck. A thin groan escaped her lips as they let her down.

"I'm sorry," John told her, "but I'm not very expert at this."

She managed a weak smile.

They stopped at the ranch house long enough to tell the wrangler where the horses were so he could send someone out for them and had him phone the hospital that they were coming in. The doctor, who had been alerted, came to the back door to meet them and directed that Aunt Abigail be taken to the emergency room.

"I know you have to do your duty," she said crisply, "but I want you to understand that I'm much too busy to lie around in this hospital of yours. So do what you've got to do, and we'll go back to the ranch."

The doctor surveyed her calmly. He had known her for a long while. "Abigail, you had just as well quit trying to give me orders. Lie back and take it easy for a while. Okay? We'll examine you and see whether you need hospitalization or not."

Apprehension appeared in Mrs. Chandler's eyes. "You know I'm much too busy to stay in the hospital, doctor. There are a dozen things I ought to be doing right now."

He nodded cryptically. "You should've thought of that before you let that horse spook and throw you off." He continued to work as he talked. "Frankly, I'm surprised at you."

He had the nurses take her into the X-ray room. It was an hour later before he returned.

"Didn't find anything broken, did you?"

He shook his head. "You must be tougher than I thought you were, Abigail. There aren't any broken bones."

"Good." She spoke with finality. "Then I can go home tonight."

"I didn't say that. You've got a severely wrenched hip that's going to have to be taken care of."

She groaned her dismay. "I might've known you'd find some excuse to keep me in this bed."

"If you don't take it easy on me, I'll keep you here for a month."

"You wouldn't dare!" Her gaze met his defiantly.

"But I don't think you'll have to stay that long. It'll be more like three weeks."

She stared at him. "Three weeks?" she echoed. "It might as well be a year!"

He hesitated, looking down to keep her from reading his eyes. "How do two weeks sound to you?"

"That's better," she admitted. "But two weeks. Two whole weeks in bed! I've got a ranch to run!"

"I know all about you and that run-down ranch of yours." He stopped momentarily. "The best I can do is overnight, Abigail. Does that suit you any better?"

She relaxed, grinning. "You old fraud! You just did that to see me squirm!"

"Abigail," he said. "How you talk!"

She turned to the girls and John. "I'll be expecting you to be back for me early in the morning. In spite of what Dr. Milner says, I've got a lot of work to do."

Twyla met the truck as they drove into the yard and stopped. Her lips curled as she saw Joan and Felicia with John, but she said nothing about that.

"How is Aunt Abigail?" she asked.

Felicia told her.

"She was lucky she didn't get a broken hip," Twyla said. "She could have been laid up for weeks."

"We were talking with your aunt about that, Twyla," Felicia said. "And we don't believe it was luck. God was watching over her."

Briefly Twyla flinched. Then a faint, cynical smile

played on her lips. "You're overplaying that religion of yours a bit, aren't you?"

The next morning, Twyla got John to go with her to town to get her aunt. Sherman was getting the wheelchair out of the back when the ranch foreman came hurrying up.

"Abigail," he said, "I've got to talk to you."

Her gaze met his. "Yes?"

"Alone."

"If you'll help me get into that contraption John's bringing," she told him, "we'll go into the office."

With Sherman's help, Pete got the wheelchair and Aunt Abigail up the steps and into her office. He waited until the door was closed. Then he turned to her.

"Abigail, I don't like to have to tell you this," he began, "especially when you just got out of the hospital this morning. But there's another mare gone."

Concern marred her face. "What happened, Pete?"

"What happened?" he exploded. "What happened the other two times? The horse is gone. That's all there is to it." He shook his head in bewilderment.

"I wish you'd tell me what happened. Then we'd both know."

He took a deep breath.

"I talked to Sheriff Getty," he said. "He wanted to know if I'd checked the fences. I told him I had my best men check those fences – every foot of them. They not only are up and in good shape, but we couldn't find a single place where it looked as though the staples had been pulled to put the wires down." He shook his head. "I'll tell you, Mrs. Chandler, I've been the foreman on this ranch for over twenty years, and I have never had anything like this happen before. It's the biggest mystery we've had to cope with."

She was silent momentarily. "What are you going to do, Pete?"

"The sheriff and a deputy or two are coming out this afternoon to look around. And in the meantime, I'm going to start keeping the horses we've got left locked in the barn. If we lose any more, we might just as well forget about training polo ponies. Nobody will trust us with them."

When he was gone, Aunt Abigail wheeled the chair out to the lounge to find Felicia and Joan.

"I don't want to shoulder my troubles onto you," she said, "but there are times when it helps just to talk to someone."

Felicia nodded understandingly. "Is there anything we can do to help?"

Aunt Abigail hesitated.

"We'd be glad to."

"I know, but I don't like to have you spend all your vacation helping me."

"Nonsense," Felicia told her. "If there's anything we can do, we want you to tell us."

There was a short silence.

"Well, if I weren't in this wheelchair, I'd ride out in that pasture and look around as carefully as I could.

I think there must be some clues that Pete and the hands are missing."

"And you'd like us to do that for you. Is that it?"

Abigail smiled. "If you don't mind, I'd certainly appreciate it."

Joan was not surprised when Felicia told her what Mrs. Chandler wanted them to do.

"I knew you would be getting us involved in this thing sooner or later," she said.

The girls were going out the door when Twyla came over to them.

"Going out for a ride?" she asked.

Felicia nodded. "Want to go along?"

"I suppose I might as well," the other girl said. "John's going to be busy this afternoon."

They had the wrangler saddle horses for them and rode into the west pasture once again.

"Looking for something special?" Twyla asked with feigned carelessness, as though she were only making conversation.

The girls did not answer her immediately.

"Not really," Joan said after a time. "Aunt Abigail just wanted us to come out and look around to see if we can find any clues the men missed. But we aren't looking for anything special."

"In fact," Felicia added, "we don't even know what we are looking for."

Twyla snickered. "That's a little silly, isn't it?" she

asked. "After all, if the men didn't find anything, how does she expect you to?"

"As far as I'm concerned, I'd just as soon we didn't find anything," Joan told them. "I'm very content to leave it to Sheriff Getty and the ranch foreman."

At the mention of the sheriff, Twyla jerked upright.

"Has the sheriff's office been called in?"

Something in her tone caught Felicia's interest. She eyed the other girl quizzically.

"Why?" She shot the word out suddenly.

Twyla wasn't expecting the question, and it caught her off guard. "John was wondering," she said. The instant she spoke she realized what she had done. The color crept into her cheeks. "I–I–" She started to alibi her way out of the statement she had made, but it was too late. She could tell by looking at their faces that the damage was done.

"He really didn't care one way or the other," she murmured lamely. "He was wondering if Pete was sure enough that the horses had been stolen to call in the authorities. That's all."

Felicia's gaze bore into hers. "He asked you to find out for him, didn't he?" she demanded.

Twyla's cheeks crimsoned. "What makes you say that?"

"That's a favorite trick of his. He asked us to do something for him too."

Twyla's eyes blazed. "After all, what difference

does it make if he wanted me to find out a thing or two for him? He's just curious, like we all are."

"Aunt Abigail doesn't entirely trust him," Joan said.

"That's because he's shown an interest in me." Twyla was almost in tears. "She's that way with every friend I have. She always finds something wrong with them."

Felicia changed the subject.

Although they rode for several hours, they were able to find nothing. Once or twice in the pasture, they thought they had located some tracks that could be fresh, but the ground was so hard they couldn't be sure. Besides, Pete and the hands had found hoofprints. They would have to come up with something different if they were going to find anything that would be of help to Aunt Abigail in locating the horses. When they rode back toward evening, they had found nothing.

* * *

It began to rain shortly after dinner that evening. Lightning forked in the cloud-darkened sky, and thunder rumbled ominously from clouds that hid the mountain peaks.

"I don't like a night like this," Joan said, shivering. "It makes me think of old castles and creaking doors and dungeons."

Felicia laughed. "Don't pay any attention to her,

Twyla," she said. "If you do, she'll half scare you out of your wits."

"You know what I mean," Joan told her.

Felicia, who had been standing by the dresser, turned and pushed aside the window shade to look out.

A few drops of rain had fallen to soften the ground, and thunder snapped noisily.

"Now you've got me doing it," she murmured.

Joan spoke, and she was about to turn to her when she stopped suddenly. An involuntary cry escaped her lips.

Both Twyla and Joan leaped to their feet. "What is it?"

Felicia's lower lip was trembling. "I–I just saw something!"

The girls stared at her, fear draining them of strength.

"Wh-wh-what did you see?"

"I'm not sure," Felicia faltered. "I–I couldn't quite make it out, but I thought I saw a big dark shape jump the corral fence!"

CHAPTER 6

DISCOVERY

For a moment or two, the girls stared at each other. A strange numbness took hold of them. Their faces were colorless and their eyes wide and staring.

"This–this thing you saw, Felicia," Joan said after a time, "what did it look like?"

Felicia moistened her lips and laughed shortly. "You'll never believe me if I tell you."

"Try us and see."

"I thought I saw a big black horse!"

Twyla snorted her disbelief. "A horse jumping that corral fence?" she echoed. "Do you realize how high it is?"

"I told you you wouldn't believe me."

"You can't expect anyone to believe a story like that," she scoffed. "You must have been dreaming."

"Maybe it was another of those polo ponies getting away," Joan suggested.

Twyla frowned. "Even if a horse could jump that corral fence, which it can't, there isn't a black horse on the place. So you're wrong all the way around."

"Maybe it was some black horse's ghost," Joan teased. "You know, it is that kind of a night."

"You can laugh if you want to," Felicia countered. "But I still say that I saw something."

"The question is," Joan went on, "what are we going to do about it?"

"I don't know about you, but I'm going down and tell Aunt Abigail."

Twyla opened the door. "I'm going along. This I've got to see."

Aunt Abigail's reaction was the same as Twyla's, only she was too kind to scoff at her openly.

Felicia did not back down. "You don't believe me, do you?"

"I believe that you saw something – or thought you did."

Twyla snickered.

When Felicia and Joan were alone half an hour later, she turned to her friend.

"I don't care what they say. I still think I saw a horse out there."

"That's all right, Felicia," Joan replied condescendingly. "I love you just the same–"

Felicia made a face at her. "You're just as bad as the rest of them!" Her mouth firmed. "But I'm going to prove it to all of you!"

The following morning as soon as breakfast was over, Felicia called Joan aside. "Come with me."

"Where are we going?" her friend asked, smiling archly.

"I just want to look for something, and I'd like to have you along."

"You don't think that mysterious black horse that wasn't there is going to be back in the corral, do you?"

"Never mind what I think. I want you to help me look for something."

They were almost to the barn when Joan spoke again. "Just what do you expect to find out here?" she demanded.

No answer.

"You know, they're all going to say that I'm crazy, too, if they see us out in the corral looking for the horse that isn't there."

"That's what you get for having a crazy friend like me."

Joan stopped and took hold of her friend's arm. "Oh, no, you don't. I'm not going another step until I know what this is all about."

Felicia's cheeks blushed delicately. "If you must know," she said, speaking in a whisper, "I'm looking for the hoofprints of the horse I saw last night."

Joan shook her head. "I'm sorry I asked. I'd have preferred going on thinking that you really do know what you're doing."

"You'll find out," Felicia countered. "And so will Twyla and Aunt Abigail."

They went over the corral as carefully as possible, but the ground was so hard and there were so many hoofprints Felicia couldn't find anything that even she could claim were the hoofprints of the horse she saw jump the fence, or thought she saw, she told herself ruefully. There had been so many doubters they had her doubting too.

At last Joan came over to her. "Why don't we just give up on this and forget it?"

"Nothing doing. I'm not going to admit defeat that easily." She straightened slowly, and, shading her eyes with her hand, looked out across the pasture. "You know," she continued. "That horse was so big his hoofprints would be larger than any of the others." She paused. "We ought to be able to pick it out from the others."

"I thought that's what we'd been trying to do."

"We did – on this side of the corral fence. Let's go on the other and see what we can come up with."

"All right," Joan said in resignation, "but hurry. I'm beginning to feel awfully foolish."

They crawled between the second and third rails of the wooden corral fence and began to examine the ground on the pasture side. After a moment or two, Joan cried out suddenly.

"Felicia! Come here!"

Felicia went over and stared at the hoofprint

Joan was pointing at. It was considerably larger than those of the average riding horse, and the depth of the indentation made the hoofprint seem unusual.

"Now don't tell me I haven't done you a favor!"

Felicia dropped to her hands and knees and was examining the print with care.

"It's deep at the front," she muttered, "the same as the hoofprints Mr. Weaver showed us. And he said they were made by jumping horses."

They both were staring at it.

"Now do you believe me?" Felicia asked.

Her friend did not reply.

"Felicia," she said after a moment or two. "Do you see anything strange about this hoofprint?"

Felicia shook her head. "Not exactly."

"It isn't the same as those made by the horses at the ranch. It was made by a horse without a shoe."

Felicia's eyes widened. "That's right. I was so excited about finding it that I didn't even notice." She drew herself slowly erect. "Now I know that I wasn't imagining things when I saw that big black horse jump the corral fence."

Joan drew a deep breath. "I can't say that I'm ready to buy the whole story, but I'm beginning to think you saw something."

At lunch, several hours later, the girls were sitting in the dining room with Aunt Abigail when Pete came in to talk to his employer.

"Tell us, Mr. Weaver," Joan broke in after he had

been talking with Mrs. Chandler for several minutes and it was apparent that his business with her had been concluded, "do you have any unshod horses on the ranch?"

Pete shook his head. "The first thing we do when we get a new horse is to shoe him. If we didn't, he'd go lame before the end of the first week."

Joan nodded triumphantly. "That's just what Felicia and I thought."

Aunt Abigail eyed the girls curiously. "What do you mean, my dear?"

"We found the hoofprint of an unshod horse," Joan continued. "The hoofprint of the horse Felicia saw last night."

Twyla snickered. "You mean the horse Felicia thought she saw last night."

Before Joan could reply, Pete spoke up. "It isn't at all unusual to find the hoofprint of an unshod horse around a place like this. We do everything we can to keep all of our saddle horses properly shod, but in spite of every precaution, they will often throw a shoe. The guest may not notice it and neglects to say anything about it until the horse shows up lame."

"So," Twyla added, "you haven't found the proof you thought you had when you said you saw a black horse jump that ridiculously high fence."

In spite of themselves, Pete and Aunt Abigail laughed. Felicia felt the color rising in her cheeks, and she felt knee-high to the second rung of a kitchen chair. When they left the dining room, Joan was indignant.

"That settles it!" she exclaimed. "You and I are going out and find that black horse! We're going to prove to everybody that there is such an animal!"

"I'm with you," Felicia replied, "but how are we going to do that? The men have been looking for those mares for almost two weeks and haven't found them."

"That's easy," Joan retorted. "They haven't been looking in the right places."

"How do you think we're going to be able to find them?"

Joan scowled. "I haven't quite worked that one out yet."

That afternoon, Joan and Felicia rode across the pasture on horseback. The rain had softened the ground enough so the hoofprints of the unshod horse were quite easy to follow. The animal had jumped the fence easily and headed straight for the upper reaches of the mountains.

The footprints indicated that the horse seemed to know exactly where he was going. He forded a creek that caused them a little trouble before they found his tracks up the opposite side and headed along a narrow game trail that led up one small rise and down into the ravine on the other side. The girls were so intent on finding the horse they were tracking that they were scarcely aware of the fact that time was passing until the shadows began to stretch endlessly along the ground.

Felicia reined up. "I don't think we ought to go any farther today, Joan," she said. "It's going to be dark in a little while."

Joan was not sure she was ready to leave. "We might come across him at any minute," she said, voicing her reluctance.

"I think it's best to get an early start in the morning," Felicia countered. "Then we can be sure we'll have time enough to track him until we find him."

"If this trail is still plain enough so we can follow it."

"That's a chance we'll have to take."

It was dark before they got to the pasture line, and when they reached the ranch house, everyone else had eaten. "It looks like cold beans and crackers for you and me," Joan muttered.

Felicia was still thinking about the hoofprints they had been following. "Don't say anything to anyone about what we've been doing today," she said.

"Don't worry. I don't enjoy being laughed at any more than you do."

Twyla saw them as they walked from the barn to the house and came to meet them.

"So you finally came back?" She laughed tauntingly. "Did you find your black horse?"

"Oh, no," Joan replied, "but we saw his tracks."

Twyla laughed again, loudly enough so that John could hear. He called out something about the horse before turning back to the ranch house. Felicia was glad she hadn't heard what he said.

"Well, one of these days, if you have the time, you'll have to take us out and show those hoofprints to us," Twyla continued loudly. "Then we'll all believe you."

Joan and Felicia didn't tell her what they had in mind. The next morning, they got up very early and went down to the kitchen. They bribed the cook into fixing them breakfast ahead of the others and making some sandwiches for lunch. Even with such an early start, it was almost eight o'clock when they reached the place where they had left off the night before.

"Now," Joan said, concern edging her voice, "if we can just continue to follow this trail, we'll be in business."

Felicia nodded. It was bad that they had to come back for the night and let the trail grow that much colder. A few hours could very well make the difference between finding and not finding the animal they were after.

However, it wasn't long until they were able to pick up the hoofprints again. They weren't distinct enough most of the time to have made a complete identification. However, every once in a while, they would find a complete hoofprint in bold relief, formed so perfectly there was no doubt that they were still on the right track.

The horse had been going steadily higher, but

now he made his way down into a deep ravine. At the bottom, he turned and followed it.

"I'm beginning to wonder if these prints were made by a real horse or not," Joan said, stopping to wipe the sweat from her forehead. "Maybe we're going to follow him for miles and miles and miles and then have him vanish into thin air."

Felicia laughed indulgently. "The ghosts I've seen have never left tracks," she informed her.

They continued to follow the trail. The farther they went, the more open the country became. The trees were farther apart, and there was less brush. On either side and at the back, mountain ridges towered above the valley.

"This is a different sort of place, isn't it?" Joan asked.

"This must be what they call a box canyon. There's only one way out, apparently."

"If we don't find that horse before long, we'll never find him."

Even before she finished, Joan had quit listening. She was staring straight ahead a quarter of a mile or so. Several beautiful horses were grazing along the rim of trees. And standing apart from them was a magnificent black stallion.

"We've found them!" Joan exclaimed, her breath coming in short, quick stabs. "We've found them!"

"And there's the black stallion! That must be the one I saw the other night!"

It was almost a minute before Joan could reply.

"Those other horses must be the stolen mares!"

That was the only explanation, Felicia admitted. She had heard stories about wild stallions stealing horses from the ranchers, but she never thought she would see it happen.

"I guess you've proved that there is such a thing as the black horse you saw the other night," Joan whispered.

Felicia did not reply. She was still sitting motionless when, without warning, a shot was fired over their heads.

"Joan!" she cried, dropping to her horse's neck. The jittery animal reared, and it was all she could do to keep control of him.

CHAPTER 7

DANGEROUS ROUNDUP

For the space of a heartbeat, Felicia and Joan clung desperately to their rearing, plunging horses, struggling to stay in the saddles and bring them under control.

"*Crack!*" Another rifle shot rang out. The bullet whistled over their heads.

That did it. The frightened horses whirled and bolted in the opposite direction, breaking back into the forest and along the ravine they had just left. For a moment or two, it was all Felicia could do to stay in the saddle. She clamped her knees against the leather and hung on, not entirely sure from one leap to the next whether she would be able to stay with her wild running cow pony.

Joan was having the same problem. She grabbed the saddle horn with one hand and dug her heels hard into her mount's flanks. The horse shied and almost sent Joan pitching headfirst to the ground. But, miraculously, she was able to cling to the horse in her uncertain, tossing position.

When the first wild burst of speed was over, the girls were able to saw on the reins and gradually bring the horses to a halt half a mile or more from the place where the runaways had started. Two or three minutes passed while the girls remained where they were, clinging to the saddle horns and fighting for breath. The cow ponies were standing with legs spraddled and their powerful chests heaving. Felicia released her grip on the saddle horn and reached forward to touch her mount's lathered withers. She could feel the animal's shoulder muscles trembling beneath the skin.

"There now," she murmured soothingly. "Everything's going to be all right."

Joan glanced nervously at the forest around them, as though she wasn't as sure as Felicia that everything was going to work out.

"When you get him quieted down," she muttered in an undertone, "I think I need a little soothing."

Felicia glanced at her friend's white, drawn face and laughed. "I think we both do."

"Whew!" Joan expelled her breath with a rush. "That's as close as I ever want to come to getting shot."

"You can say that again," Felicia agreed. "I certainly didn't expect anything like that."

"Neither did I."

The girls stared at each other.

"At least we know now that your black horse does exist, and we found the mares that have been disappearing from the ranch."

"The trouble is that we're not the only ones who found them," Felicia said.

For a moment or two, they paused, eyeing each other uneasily.

"If we don't do something and do it right away, the men who shot at us will catch those mares, and Aunt Abigail and their rightful owners will never see them again."

"Or," Joan added, "the stallion will move the herd and we might not be able to locate them again."

As soon as their mounts were rested, Felicia and Joan started for the ranch at a fast trot. The foreman was at the barn when the girls rode up. He listened as they breathlessly told him the things that had happened. He seemed doubtful of the story at first and questioned them closely, but at last he was satisfied.

"I guess that sort of thing is possible," he acknowledged. "I've heard some of the old-timers tell about it when there were bands of wild horses roaming these hills. But I haven't known of a wild horse around here for years."

He turned to the wrangler. "You've lived here longer than I have, Hank, can you remember hearing about any wild horses?"

"Can't say that I have, but there was that fire in the

hills, and a lot of elk and bears and deer came down. There could've been some wild horses up there too."

Pete nodded. "I'd never thought of that. Well, no matter. We've got to move and move fast if we're going to get those mares."

"Want me to saddle some horses for you?" Hank asked.

"Yeah. And get fresh mounts for the girls." He spun on his heels to face Felicia and Joan. "I'm going to have to ask you girls to ride with us. We may need you to help locate the place."

"But what about the men who shot at us?" Joan demanded.

"I'll have Hank phone the sheriff."

"A lot of help that'll be if they start shooting again before he catches up with them."

"You aren't going to have to worry about that. Whoever shot at you was only trying to frighten you away."

"You sound awfully sure of yourself," Joan countered.

"I am. A man with a high-powered rifle doesn't miss a target as large as two girls on horseback unless he does it deliberately."

Pete left before she had a chance to talk to him further.

"I don't know whether he was trying to be comforting or not," she said softly, "but he was anything but–" She shivered.

Neither Joan nor Felicia was aware that Twyla was even near the barn until she stepped out of the shadows.

"It sounds as though you had an exciting time this morning."

"It wasn't my idea of fun, if that's what you mean," Joan told her.

"I'm going with you," she announced firmly.

"You'll have to ask Mr. Weaver."

A faint, mocking smile lifted one corner of her mouth. "I won't ask him. I'll tell him." She started for the house. "Don't go away before I get back."

Twyla returned before Pete did, her phone in her hand.

"This sounds like the first real excitement since I've been here. I wouldn't miss it for anything."

The foreman scarcely gave a glance to Twyla when he returned with four or five cowhands. "All right, let's go." He jerked his head in Felicia's direction. "I want you to ride with me so you can guide us."

They rode across the pasture and up the steep slope in the direction Felicia and Joan had followed the hoofprints of the black horse. After a long period of fast trotting, they neared the box canyon where they had seen the herd.

Pete questioned Felicia closely. "We ought to be getting near the canyon," she said at last. "The trees are beginning to thin."

Pete pursed his lips.

He started to speak but checked himself and turned to one of the hands.

"Ben, didn't you used to live over this way?" he asked.

"Sure did. I've hunted elk in this canyon and the next one for the last fifteen years."

"Tell me something about it."

Ben rode over to the foreman. "Well, there are these two box canyons side by side," he began. "This is the smaller of the two. It's shaped like a bottle, and we're in the neck."

"Any way out besides this entrance?"

The cowhand shook his head. "Not that I know of. I used to like to get an elk in here because I was dead sure of getting him."

Pete nodded. "This is a stroke of luck. I didn't have any idea that we'd be able to get these horses in a place like this."

"If they're still here," Ben said laconically.

Pete turned his mount and rode on, the others a few paces behind. He had just left the trees when he reined in quickly. Half a mile ahead, the black stallion came up on a little rise and stood, head high and nostrils flaring. Behind him a hundred yards or so, the rest of the horses grazed quietly.

A tense, expectant silence gripped the small party of horsemen. Weaver stared at the magnificent animal. "Look at him!" he whispered. "Just look at him!"

Felicia pulled in a deep breath. She wanted to speak, but for the moment she could not.

"I've seen a lot of horses in my day," the ranch foreman muttered, "but I've never seen one like that!"

"How do we go about getting those mares away from him, Pete?" one of the men asked.

"Let's try to get him, too."

The cowhand laughed mirthlessly. "That's not going to be so easy. Let me clue you in."

Pete ignored the remark. "All right, fellas," he said. "Spread out and move forward slowly. Unless I miss my guess, our black friend will move the herd away from us. If we can get them back into the canyon, we can seal off the entrance, and we'll have them all."

The riders followed the foreman's orders and spread out before moving forward. While they waited for the signal to advance on the herd of horses, Joan looked in one direction and then the other.

"What are you looking up there for?" Twyla asked uneasily.

"I was just wondering if the people who shot at us were going to do the same thing again."

Felicia shuddered. "Now that's a happy thought!"

Weaver gave the signal, and they began to move forward. With the first move in his direction, the big black horse jerked to attention. His head turned slightly from left to right and back again as he eyed the riders. At first, he stood his ground, feet spraddled slightly and nostrils flaring. Just to look at him made Felicia's heart beat faster.

The big horse snorted and backed off, still keeping his eyes fixed on the row of riders moving steadily in his direction. He whinnied a note of warning, and the other horses quit eating abruptly. As he backed off, so did they, uncertainly, willing to accept his leadership but not quite understanding what was going on.

Weaver held up his hand as he reined his horse to a stop. The line halted.

"Take it easy," the foreman said softly to the cowhands on either side. "We don't want to panic that old boy, or he'll come blasting through us and take the herd with him."

The wild horse stopped when they stopped, but he continued to eye them warily. The herd began to graze once more. When that happened, Weaver motioned the men forward. They moved with caution, a few steps at a time.

The magnificent black fiddle-footed nervously. For the space of a heartbeat, Felicia thought he was going to come charging straight for them. But he did not. Instead, he whirled and dashed back into the canyon, the others at his heels.

"Come on!" the foreman shouted, kicking his own pony into a fast gallop. "Keep moving! Keep the pressure on!"

The canyon was so narrow by this time that a

strong man could have thrown a rock across it. Weaver brought his men to a halt.

"Looks like we've got them, boss," one of the men said exultantly.

But Pete was not so sure. "With a horse like that, we haven't got him until we've got a rope on him and have him in a stall. Even then, you won't be sure of him!"

He glanced quickly around. Their moves were going to have to be exactly right. Men could be stationed at intervals across the narrow neck of the canyon. There would be no chance for the stallion to get past them. The left flank was a sheer granite cliff. The right was not so formidable, but it, too, presented an acceptable barrier. The first rise was fifty or sixty feet high and on the canyon side was too steep for a horse to climb.

"Ben," Pete ordered, "take three men into the canyon after him. I'll stay here with the rest to turn him back in case he gets by you. Okay. You three come with me."

As they moved out, the foreman glanced in the girls' direction. "I want you girls to go around to the other side and get on that high spot. And whatever happens, stay there."

A pout formed on Twyla's pretty young face. "But Pete, I want to get some pictures."

"Fine. You get all the pictures you want but stay up there where you won't get hurt."

"Get hurt?" she echoed. "How could we possibly get hurt?"

He did not reply.

Although Twyla objected strenuously to going up where the foreman said for them to go, she followed his orders without further objection. From their point of vantage, the girls watched the stallion move the small herd back into the canyon. He did so with growing uncertainty – turning now and again to face the men who were forcing him into a corner.

Twyla focused her camera on it. "I wish Pete would have let us go with them," she complained. "I'm too far away to get a good picture."

Felicia and Joan were watching the tense scene breathlessly.

The horses moved reluctantly back into the canyon under the relentless pressure of the men. At last, they could go no further. They came to a halt, and the stallion whirled defiantly, eyes red with anger and nostrils flaring. There was no fear in him as he waited. The riders, lariats in hand, continued to move cautiously forward. They, too, tensed, knowing that the moment of encounter was not far away.

The big horse reared, screaming his challenge, and catapulted toward the waiting riders. Ropes snaked out as he charged close, but the stallion seemed to have the uncanny knack of throwing his head or dodging at the right instant. The loops fell harmlessly away.

The cowhands did what they could to hold the

herd but were unprepared for the sudden fury of the attack. The men under Ben's direction could not contain the angered stallion.

The huge black stallion dashed straight for one of the men, as unerringly as a bullet. The cowboy's horse screamed in terror and almost threw his rider in his frantic haste to avoid the violent charge. The entire herd broke through the opening.

"Look out, Pete!" Ben shouted. "They're coming!"

But there was no need for the warning. The foreman had already seen what was happening. This time the advantage was with the men. The mouth of the canyon was narrow, and the riders had time to get set for the hard-running herd.

The stallion charged the line, but, this time, the rider held his mount in check and snaked out his loop. It may have been the rope that turned him – or it may have been that the horse and rider did not give way, but turn he did. He braked and whirled in one effortless motion. The rest of the herd turned back.

"Get him!" Pete shouted. "Get him!"

Two riders thundered after the stallion. The big horse whirled again, saw that the mouth of the canyon was closed, and hesitated. The riders narrowed the distance to him. Only then did he seem to panic, realizing the seriousness of his situation. He reared, turned on his hind legs, and charged desperately up the steep slope directly at the three girls.

"Look out!" Felicia shouted.

Twyla's mount almost fell as it scrambled to one side when the stallion clawed his way up the steep slope in great, bounding leaps and thundered past.

Below, the hands recovered their composure enough to seal off the canyon again and hold the small herd of mares. Once the stallion was gone, it was obvious that the rest of them were not wild horses. They ran back and forth a few times but soon came quivering to a halt.

"All right, men," Weaver ordered, "let's get ropes on these horses. We don't want to take a chance on losing any of them."

"What about that black rascal?" one of the men demanded.

"We'll take care of him later."

While they were busy, Felicia turned to Twyla. "Are you all right?"

The other girl was still white and shaken. She opened her mouth to speak but stopped and pointed to the sheer cliff that dropped away some sixty or eighty feet.

"My horse almost went over that cliff," she stammered. "I–I could've been killed."

Felicia nodded. "God was watching over you," she replied.

Twyla's gaze met hers. "That's a strange thing to say."

"I don't think so. Both Joan and I know what it is

to have God take care of us in times of trouble and danger, don't we?"

Joan nodded.

"I've never figured God cared much about what I did," Twyla said, laughing nervously.

"That's where you're wrong. The Bible says He loves you so much He sent His Son to die on the cross for you."

Twyla stared at her. "I can't buy that religion of yours," she said curtly. With that she neck-reined her horse to turn him and rode away.

CHAPTER 8

MORE TROUBLE

Felicia, Joan, and Twyla waited until the men had rounded up the last of the expensive polo ponies and were ready to start back to the ranch with them. Once that had been accomplished, Pete rode over to where the girls were waiting.

"Some show, eh?" He grinned his relief.

"It was exciting, all right," Joan said.

Felicia eyed him triumphantly. "Now will you believe that I saw that black horse jump the corral fence?"

"I apologize to you, young lady. I'll believe anything anybody ever tells me about that black horse from now on. I don't believe there's another horse like him in all of Colorado."

"Where do you think he came from?" Joan asked.

The foreman glanced up at the ridge above them.

"All I can think of is that he's been up in the hills

somewhere until he was forced down here by the forest fire this spring." He paused, and a wistful tone crept into his voice. "But I can tell you this much. I'd give a lot to own him."

They started moving the horses down the narrow cut, and, at last, to the pasture.

"We'll leave them here," Pete said.

Ben, his straw boss, stared at him. "Are you out of your mind, Pete? That black demon isn't going to give up that easily. He'll be back. We're just asking for this sort of trouble all over again."

Pete nodded. "That's exactly what I'm hoping will happen. I want to put these mares in the pasture for bait and set a guard over them. When he comes back for them, we'll have another chance to get him."

"All right," Ben said, shaking his head, "but I think you're out of your mind."

The sheriff was waiting for them when they got back to the ranch to question them about the shooting.

"Did you see anyone?" he asked.

Felicia shook her head. "But we certainly heard the bullets whine over us."

His eyes narrowed.

"You couldn't have been mistaken about that?"

"They were bullets, all right. Both of us heard them."

"Maybe someone set off a charge of dynamite," the sheriff suggested.

"I've heard dynamite plenty of times," Joan retorted. "It wasn't that."

"But it could have been a poacher who mistook you for a deer or an elk."

Felicia thought about that. It didn't seem likely to her. Yet she couldn't be positive that it wasn't.

The sheriff continued his questioning, but it was obvious that he didn't believe anyone had shot at them. Not deliberately, that is.

"Well," he said at last, "I'll ride up that way one of these times and look around."

Although the ranch foreman put the mares back in the main pasture where the stallion had first come for them and posted a guard twenty-four hours a day, the big horse did not return.

"I can't understand it, Mrs. Chandler," he said. "I thought that horse would have been right back down here."

"Maybe he was frightened enough when you almost captured him to keep him from coming back," Joan said.

Pete did not agree. "There's got to be some reason for it, but that isn't it. He isn't afraid of anything."

"Well," Aunt Abigail said quickly, "we're not going to worry about him. We got our mares back. That's the most important thing."

The following morning, the three girls were coming out of their room for breakfast when Aunt Abigail wheeled her chair down the hall.

"Oh, there you are," she said. "I've been trying to find you."

"Is there something wrong?"

She tried to continue, but it was a moment or two before she could. Her face was white, and her hands, on either arm of the wheelchair, were trembling.

"I just came from my office," she said slightly above a whisper. "Somebody has broken into it!"

Felicia gasped. "Did they steal anything?"

"That's just it," the older woman said. "Right now, I can't find anything that's been taken. But, fortunately, I don't keep money in the office."

"Maybe the thief came in and got frightened away," Twyla said.

"Oh, no," her aunt countered. "The mess my office is in, he couldn't have been frightened away. He must have been in there for hours! He has been through everything!"

Aunt Abigail turned her wheelchair around quickly and led the girls down the corridor. "And what's more," she said crisply, "John is gone!"

Twyla straightened quickly. "That can't be!" she exclaimed, hurt leaping to her eyes. "He told me that he's going to be here until the end of the week."

"You can go to his room if you like," Aunt Abigail said, "and see for yourself. He left payment for his bill and a note saying he was sorry he had to go, but something had come up unexpectedly, and he didn't want to waken me."

Twyla looked as though she had been slapped.

"John didn't do it," she murmured lamely. "He wouldn't steal anything."

"Don't be too sure of that," Aunt Abigail murmured.

Anger smoked in her niece's eyes. "Aunt Abigail!" she exploded. "How can you say such a thing?"

Her aunt muttered something under her breath and turned her wheelchair. "Don't go in the office," she warned. "I called the sheriff, and he said we shouldn't touch anything. He'll be out here in a few minutes."

Two officers came out from the county seat and went over Aunt Abigail's office carefully.

"I don't mind coming out for something like this," he said. "What I don't like is to have to come every time some rancher has a steer or a couple of horses stray off." He glanced at Felicia and her two companions. "Or some greenhorn thinks a bandit is shooting at him."

The girls colored but did not argue with him.

He continued his investigation of the office.

"It's strange there's nothing missing," he said after a time. "Are you sure you didn't have anything else in the office, Abigail? Something you might have forgotten? Something they could have stolen?"

She pursed her lips and thought a minute. "I can't imagine what it would be," she said. "I don't keep anything of importance here – just the books and the papers we need to carry on the business of the ranch."

The sheriff pulled out a chair and sat down. "Have

you looked through your papers to see if anything is missing?"

With the girls helping, Aunt Abigail checked the papers that had been strewn about the floor. The books were all there, recording the financial matters of the ranch operations. So were the papers that dealt with Mr. Chandler's estate. At last, they finished.

"Well, how about it?" the sheriff asked. "Did you find everything?"

"As far as I know, there's nothing missing at all. Except for the registration papers of Nugget."

Interest kindled in the officer's eyes. "And who's Nugget?"

"The little stallion we bought a little while before my husband died." She paused. "But Nugget was killed, and there's no reason anyone would want the papers on a dead horse."

Felicia spoke up. "Are you sure Nugget was killed, Aunt Abigail?" she asked.

The ranch owner eyed her quizzically. "Didn't I tell you? He went over the edge of a cliff in a horse trailer. He was killed instantly."

"But did you see his body?" the girl persisted. "Do you know positively that he was killed?"

Abigail bristled. "One of our men buried him. Why?"

"I was thinking about that big black stallion that stole the mares. Mr. Weaver said he's the most beautiful horse he'd ever seen, and you were telling us that Nugget was the best colt your husband could find."

"It couldn't be him." Aunt Abigail said stiffly. "It's out of the question."

Twyla leaned forward suddenly. "Aunt Abigail, do you remember what he looked like?"

"Perfectly."

"I'll be right back."

"I don't know what all this has to do with my office," the sheriff said, getting to his feet. "I'll take a look around outside and go back to town to write up my report. Get in touch with me if there are any new developments."

He passed Twyla just outside the office door. She came running into the room, her phone in her hand. "I just remembered that when that big black horse came charging up the hill toward us, I was about to take a picture. I don't know whether I got it or not."

The girls crowded close. Twyla had taken the picture, but she must have done so just as her own horse jumped. The picture was so blurred all she could tell was that she was photographing a horse.

"I might've known it."

Aunt Abigail squinted at the picture.

"I can't tell by this one way or the other, but I know Nugget was killed. The insurance adjuster had his body dug up to look at him."

The girls went to their room.

"You know," Felicia said, "I'm not convinced yet

that Nugget is dead. The black stallion came right up to the barn. That means he's not afraid of people and could mean that he hasn't always been wild."

The corners of Twyla's mouth tightened. "I hadn't thought of that, but you could be right."

Joan nodded. "And the worst of it is that you'll probably die of curiosity because we'll never be able to find out for sure."

Felicia went to the window and for a long while stared out across the valley. "You know," she said abruptly, "I'm afraid we're missing something here. There was that guy shooting at us the other day, for one thing."

"According to the sheriff, that could have been done by a poacher who mistook us for an elk."

"I know what he said, but I don't believe that, and I don't think you do, either."

"If it is true, his eyes were sure bad. That's all I can say."

"Then there's this black stallion who isn't afraid of people even though he's running wild and the robbery in the ranch office."

Joan's eyes lighted. "And," she added, "the only thing that was stolen was the papers for the little stallion Aunt Abigail said was killed."

"But if he was killed," Twyla put in, "why would anyone want the papers?"

"Maybe she just thought he was killed," Felicia went on. "Maybe–"

"There are a lot of things that don't make sense in this," Joan said, "but I can see what you're driving at, Felicia. Everything that's happened does seem to tie together in some way."

"Even the fact that John left in the middle of the night – the very night the ranch office was broken into."

Twyla faced her, eyes blazing. "You know John didn't have anything to do with that robbery, Felicia! Just because he wouldn't show any interest in you and wanted to be with me, you can't accuse him of breaking into Aunt Abigail's office."

"That's very true. But you've got to admit that it does look suspicious."

"I don't know." She drew herself up archly. "I have confidence in him," she said. "I know that when he comes back, he'll have a logical explanation for everything that has happened."

Twyla went off by herself. When she came back an hour or so later, it was obvious that she had been crying. Felicia and Joan thought she would be angry with them. Quite the contrary, she was as pleasant as she had ever been – only a bit quieter and withdrawn.

"We've been thinking about going out for a ride, Twyla," Joan told her. "Would you like to go along?"

She smiled briefly. "Where are you going? Out to see if you can catch a glimpse of that black horse again?"

Felicia nodded. "There has to be some reason why

he hasn't come around, and Mr. Weaver and the men are too busy right now to go out and look for him."

"Maybe he went back where he came from," Twyla said. "Maybe he's back in the high country a long way from the ranch."

"And," Joan added, "maybe the guy who shot at us got him."

"Don't say that, Joan," Felicia broke in. "Don't even think it! If he went back into the hills where nobody can get to him, that's one thing. If he is penned up by someone who'll be mean to him, I–I won't be able to stand it."

The girls went down to the barn and asked the wrangler to saddle horses for them.

CHAPTER 9

CAPTURED

The girls rode across the pasture and up the steep mountain slope in the direction of the box canyon where they had found the black stallion and the polo ponies. They talked about many things, but Twyla entered into the conversation only when one of the other girls asked her a direct question.

After a time, she turned to Felicia. "You don't think John would break into Aunt Abigail's office, do you?"

"I'd hate to think he would," Felicia answered.

"But he's so-so nice."

"That doesn't always mean a person's honest," Felicia went on. "And we do have to admit that he did some strange things."

Twyla's face was white and drawn. "I–I–" The words choked in her mouth, and she could not speak.

They rode to the place where they had seen the

big horse and up to the cliff. For a time, they looked intently about but could not see him anywhere.

"I don't know why we'd think he would stay around here," Felicia said. "He's probably a hundred miles away by this time."

"We can't forget that somebody else knows about the black stallion too," Joan said.

"But Pete and the men are busy," Twyla put in. "They couldn't have caught him."

"You're forgetting the men who shot at us."

She shivered and glanced apprehensively about.

"They could have been watching us, and when the stallion got away from us, they could have taken after him," Joan continued. "They'd have a better chance than we would have had too. He was all tired out."

Felicia drew in a deep breath. "We'd just as well go," she said. "I don't think we've got any chance of finding him."

They were about to leave the cliff when Joan saw a thin gray spiral of smoke in the sky.

"I didn't know anyone lived over here," she said.

"Nobody does," Twyla retorted.

"There's somebody over there." She indicated the smoke with a jerk of the head.

"It couldn't be hunters this time of year," Twyla said, "and I've never heard of campers getting so far from the main road."

"Maybe it's our little friends with the rifle."

Felicia's eyes gleamed. "Do you suppose it is?"

"It's just about got to be." Joan recognized the look on her friend's face. "Wait a minute. Just what have you got in mind?"

"I was just thinking that we could go over there and see if they have caught him."

"Now that's a great idea. I can just see us riding up to that rifle-shooting character and saying, 'Pardon me, but I think you've got a horse here that belongs to the Chandler ranch. Mind if we look around?'"

"I didn't quite figure on doing it like that."

"However you figure on doing it, it's no good. Let me clue you in."

"All I want to do is to get close enough to see whether they've got him or not."

"It won't make any difference one way or another," Twyla said. "A wild horse belongs to anybody who can put a rope on him."

"But only if he's a wild horse," Felicia reminded her. "If that stallion happens to be Nugget, he belongs to Aunt Abigail."

The girls talked it over and finally decided to ride toward the smoke in an effort to see where it came from.

"But we're not going close enough to get into any trouble," Joan said. "I can tell you that right now."

"Agreed."

They followed a narrow game trail to the bottom of the ravine. There they turned at right angles, climbing up the opposite slope. The trail led almost to the top of the ridge before circling the rocky peaks and starting down.

Felicia reined in momentarily. "We're looking down on that other box canyon," she said. "I had no idea it was so close."

"And there's the cabin the smoke is coming from."

"That settles that," Felicia said, disappointment coloring her voice. "The smoke's coming from somebody's summer cabin. That horse won't be down there."

Twyla wasn't so sure. "If there was a summer place over here, I think the men would have mentioned it," she countered. "The way they talked, nobody lived over this way."

Joan stood in the stirrups and peered intently in the direction of the smoke. "It's just possible that the men we're looking for are staying down there," she said. "They could have appropriated somebody's old cabin for a while."

Excitement gleamed in Felicia's eyes. "You just might have something there." She rode forward a few paces. "I wish I had some binoculars."

"I've got some," Twyla exclaimed.

"Good! Take a look at that clearing and see if you can make out anything that looks unusual."

"Like a big black stallion in the barn," Joan added.

A grin teased the corners of Twyla's mouth. "I forgot to tell you. My binoculars are back in our room at the ranch."

"Great," Joan said. "Run back and get them. We'll wait for you."

"On second thought, they must be back home," Twyla said, laughing.

For a moment, the girls sat motionless in their saddles.

"What are we going to do?" Twyla asked in a coarse whisper.

"We've got to get closer," Joan whispered. "We can't find out anything from here."

For answer, Felicia dismounted and started to tie her horse to a clump of scrub brush.

Joan eyed her with growing concern.

"Now what?" she asked suspiciously.

"We can do it better on foot."

"If they see us, we'll never make it without our horses. They'll nab us before we can move a hundred yards."

"They're not going to see us," Felicia informed her.

Joan shook her head in resignation. "You're going to get me in real trouble yet."

Twyla followed their actions reluctantly. She swung to the ground and tied her mount beside those of Felicia and Joan.

"Now what do we do?" she whispered.

"We'll go along this trail until we get close enough to see what is going on down there," Felicia told her.

With that, she started forward stealthily, keeping on the game trail. Although a second trail led to the floor of the canyon from where they stood, they kept to the top of the ridge. Even though they were half a mile from the cabin, they moved as quietly as possible, placing one foot ahead of the other with care. Their lithe young bodies tensed as they drew closer, and they were even more cautious about giving away their presence to anyone who might happen to be nearby.

After a time, they reached a place where they could see the buildings plainly. Joan grasped Felicia's arm.

"What did I tell you? It is an old run-down place, after all."

Felicia nodded.

Twyla's breath was coming in quick, shallow gasps. "Haven't we seen enough?" she asked, scarcely mouthing the words. "Let's go back."

But Felicia didn't hear her. "There's a corral," she whispered, excitement tightening her voice. "If we go a little farther, we'll be able to see whether they've got the black horse in there or not."

"I don't see how they could've caught him," Joan said, "when we couldn't."

Another half a dozen steps and Felicia stopped, gasping aloud.

"There he is!" she exclaimed under her breath. "They did get him after all!"

The beautiful black horse was standing in one corner of the dilapidated corral, two lariats on him – one tied to the snubbing post and the other to the fence. Even that was not enough to keep him from rearing and striking the air savagely with his front hooves. As he did so, he screamed defiance. The sound of it floated up to where the girls were crouching.

"The poor animal," Felicia murmured. "I was in hopes that they wouldn't get him."

"So was I," Joan said. "They must have caught him the day he got away from Mr. Weaver and the men."

Twyla touched Felicia's elbow.

"That takes care of that," she said softly. "We might as well go now."

Felicia did not move. "Shouldn't we send back for Mr. Weaver?" she asked.

"What good would that do? A wild horse belongs to whoever catches him, and those guys caught him."

"But if he is Aunt Abigail's Nugget, he'd belong to her, wouldn't he?"

While they were discussing the matter, the cabin door opened, and a man stepped out.

Twyla cried out involuntarily. "John!"

There in the yard stood John Sherman!

CHAPTER 10

WITNESSES

Twyla's face was white and drawn, and her breath was coming in quick, short stabs. She picked up a twig and began to twist it nervously between her fingers. For the space of a minute or two, Felicia was afraid she was going to cry.

"Th-there's got to be some good reason for this," she said, fighting to control her emotions. "John isn't that kind. He's not going to be doing something that isn't right."

"I don't know," Joan retorted brusquely. "He sure wanted to get his hands on a certain stallion. He acted to me as though he'd have done most anything to get him."

Twyla's lips quivered. "You only say that because you don't know him."

"I don't know him very well," Felicia said, "and I

don't have any idea what he's doing down there, but whatever it is, he seems to be in a big hurry."

"He isn't doing anything wrong," Twyla repeated lamely. "I don't care what you say."

While they watched, two other men came out of the cabin. They built a small fire in the corral and thrust something into it.

"What are they doing?" Felicia asked curiously.

"Heating a branding iron." Twyla's voice caught. "They're going to brand him."

A gasp escaped Felicia's lips.

"And whoever gets a brand on him will own him," Twyla said. "It's proof of ownership unless it can be proved that the brand was tampered with."

Felicia's mouth tightened. "I still think that horse belongs to Aunt Abigail," she said firmly.

"Maybe – but how are we going to prove it?"

"I don't know, but we've got to do something."

For a moment, the only sound was that of the wind rustling through the trees.

"Do you think we can get a little closer?" Felicia asked.

"As far as I'm concerned, we're plenty close enough."

Felicia began to move down the game trail, and her companions followed cautiously. They went along the ridge three or four hundred yards and then began to move down, one step at a time, picking their way between the aspen and spruce that covered the sides of the canyon in a dense growth.

"Don't you think we're close enough?" Joan whispered tensely.

"We can't see a thing from here."

"We can go back where we came from," her friend muttered. "We could see from there, all right."

Felicia held a finger to her lips in warning and began to move forward.

By the time they reached the place where they had an unrestricted view of the corral, they were within a hundred yards of the building. Only then did Felicia stop.

"We'd better get out of here," Joan whispered in warning. "They'll catch us for sure."

"Not if we keep quiet." Felicia parted the brush cautiously to see what was going on in the corral.

John was still crouched beside the fire, holding an iron in it while the other two advanced gingerly on the big black stallion they had tied in the corral. The horse did not move. There was no fear in him of the two men who moved so reluctantly toward him. His gaze was fixed boldly on them. Another step, and his head came up, and his ears flattened back.

"Oh!" Twyla gasped as that happened.

One of the men saw it too. "Look out, Charlie! That ugly brute means business!"

They both stopped.

John drew the iron from the fire and looked at it. "When do you know if this iron's hot enough?" he shouted.

Twyla gasped again.

"What's the matter?" Joan demanded.

No answer.

"What is it? What's wrong?"

"There's got to be some mistake," Twyla whispered to herself. "It can't be true!"

"Whatever are you talking about?" Felicia whispered.

"That isn't a regular branding iron," she managed. "It's called a running iron."

That didn't mean anything to her companions.

"What's a running iron?"

It was difficult for Twyla to go on. "A regular branding iron is made in the shape of the brand – whatever it is. It's heated and put on the animal. A running iron is a straight piece that–that's used to change brands."

At first, they didn't get the significance.

"What's so bad about that?"

"Don't you see? A brand is proof of ownership."

Felicia's eyes gleamed. "I get it now! That means the horse already has a brand on him and they're planning on changing it!"

Twyla nodded. "It looks as though the horse belongs to Aunt Abigail after all."

The men who had been advancing in the direction of the black stallion backed off.

"I don't care what you say, Charlie," the other

exclaimed. "I wouldn't try to put another loop on that animal for ten thousand dollars."

Charlie swore. "He's already got two ropes on him to keep him from getting at us. All we've got to do is get another or two around his legs and throw him so we can go to work on that brand."

"That's *all* there is to it. You make it sound as though it's as simple as branding a calf."

"You knew what he was before you agreed to come along," Charlie reminded him darkly.

"No, I didn't! And neither did you! Nobody could know one horse could be that mean! Or that smart!" He laid down his rope and walked back to the corral fence. "If you want him roped, hop to it. Rope him yourself. I'm through!"

Charlie laughed. "Don't get so worked up! We've got the tranquilizer gun. We can always use that on him."

John spoke up. "That's to be a last resort. Remember? We're not going to take unnecessary chances with him. It's dangerous to use dosage as strong as that."

"Listen, buster," the first man put in, "it's dangerous to go over there and try to get that beast on the ground without tranquilizers. Believe me."

John continued to object, but the other two men paid no attention to him.

"Get the stuff, Sam," Charlie said. "We'll use it."

The girls looked at one another helplessly.

"What are we going to do?" Joan whispered.

Felicia shrugged expressively.

Twyla whispered, "My phone is in my saddle bags. I–I could try to–to get a picture." Her voice faltered.

Felicia nodded. "Good idea."

At that, Twyla started back up the trail.

Charlie rigged up the tranquilizer gun and went around behind the big horse to shoot him in the rump with it. The stallion flinched as the dart stuck in him.

"There," Sam exclaimed, relief evident in his voice, "that's going to be better. All we've got to do is to wait for him to go to sleep. Then we can do what we want to with him."

At first, there was no change in the animal. His head remained high, alert for every movement about him. But that was only until the powerful drug went to work. The animal's head lowered slightly, and his powerful body began to relax.

Charlie, who was watching every change in the big horse, motioned Sam forward. "Better get those ropes loosened. He's goin' down in a minute."

Sam edged forward and reached out to touch the rope that was around the snubbing post. As he did so, the horse's knees sagged. Sam freed the end of the lariat an instant before the rope tightened.

When the horse went down, the men sprang into action.

"Get those hobbles and the halter!" Charlie cried. "And bring me that iron!"

Felicia and Joan were staring helplessly at the scene below them.

"If Twyla doesn't get back in a jiffy," Joan said, "it's not going to do any good."

Felicia turned and glanced upward. It was a long way back to the place where they had tied their horses. It might take her another ten minutes to get back. And by that time, it would be too late. There had to be something she could do. But what?

While the girls crouched there, the men put a halter on the horse in addition to the two ropes and hobbles to keep him from running should he get away.

The horse's leg jerked.

"Hurry with that branding iron!" Sam cried. "He's coming around!"

John started for the big black stallion, the running iron in his hand. He held the iron out to Charlie.

"Here you are," he said. "I understand you're the artist with this thing."

At that instant, Felicia stood upright. Joan gasped aloud and grabbed for her hand in an effort to jerk her back out of sight. But it was too late.

"John!" Felicia cried.

The men froze. For half a heartbeat, they didn't even look around. Then their heads jerked in Felicia's direction.

"John!" she shouted again. "Smile pretty so you'll look nice when Twyla takes your picture!"

The men stopped what they were doing suddenly.

John dropped the running iron as though it had come alive.

Felicia hadn't finished speaking before she whirled and scrambled upward through the thick growth of spruce. Joan was right behind her. In their haste, they forgot the trail. They forgot everything except that John and the others knew they had been spying on them.

"Don't move!" John shouted, suddenly finding his voice. With that, he bounded after them. "Don't move another step, or it'll go bad for you!"

"It–it's bad enough already," Joan panted hoarsely. "We can't take a chance on them getting us!"

"Come on!" Felicia said under her breath.

For the moment, Felicia and Joan thought he must have given up the chase, but that hope was soon destroyed.

"Sherman!" Charlie bawled, his voice taut with emotion. "Come back here!"

"It's just a couple of girls!" the young man shouted over his shoulder. "They can't cause us any trouble if we catch them before they get back to the ranch with that picture."

He continued up the steep slope. Felicia was running as hard as she could. She slipped once and went sprawling, tearing a three-cornered piece out of her shirt. Joan stopped long enough to help her get to her feet, and they kept pushing upward.

"Don't be a fool, Sherman!" the older man rasped.

"The whole ball of wax is in the fire now. We've got to beat it, or we'll have the law on us!"

"You can let 'em get away with this if you want to, but I'm not goin' to!" By this time, he had reached the trees and was pursuing the girls noisily. "I'm goin' to catch them if it's the last thing I ever do."

"It won't do no good to chase after him, Sam," Charlie exclaimed. "Let the crazy galoot go. Start the car. If he wants to spend a couple of years in the pen, that's his business. We're clearin' out!"

With that, John must have come to a halt. The sound of crackling twigs and brush stopped abruptly.

"Wait up!" he called. "Wait for me!"

The car engine started.

"Wait, I tell you!"

Felicia and Joan heard the sound of running footsteps. This time they were going in the opposite direction. They stopped running themselves and crouched behind a clump of aspen, breathing heavily.

"Snap it up!" Sam cried, hysteria marring his shrill voice. "We ain't got all day."

"What about the horse?"

"What about him?" Charlie echoed. "We ain't got a chance of gettin' away with him now!"

The car door slammed. An instant later, the engine roared as the vehicle turned sharply and began to bounce over the narrow twisting road that led out of the canyon to the highway forty miles to the east.

CHAPTER 11

MYSTERY SOLVED

Only then did Felicia turn to her companion. "Well," she said in a choked voice, "they're gone!"

Joan straightened, her eyes fixed on her friend.

"They're gone," she said, "but I thought you were out of your ever-lovin' mind! What made you do such a crazy thing, anyway?"

"I had to do something, or they'd have gotten away with that beautiful horse of Aunt Abigail's."

"You almost cost us our necks." Joan shivered. "I hate to think what would have happened if John had caught us. Was he mad!"

They were still talking when Twyla came rushing down to them, her phone in her hand.

"What happened?" she demanded. "What's been going on?"

"Felicia likes to live dangerously," Joan said. "That's all. "I'm warning you, Twyla. If you want to stay well and not get scared out of your wits every time you turn around, don't make friends with Felicia. She'll be the ruin of you."

Twyla looked from one to the other. "Will one of you please tell me what this is all about?"

"Felicia stood up and told John to say 'cheese', so we'd have a good picture of him. That's all."

"But I had the camera," Twyla protested.

A faint grin lifted one corner of Felicia's mouth. "But John and his friends didn't know that. Besides, I didn't tell him we had a camera right then."

"I guess that's right, but he sure reacted. I thought he was going to catch us and crack our heads together."

At the mention of John, Twyla's young face clouded. For a brief time, her lips quivered as though she was once more on the verge of tears.

"Wh-what do we do now?" she asked.

"Go back to the ranch and tell Mr. Weaver that we know where we can get that black stallion," Felicia said.

* * *

Pete was at the ranch when the girls rode in. He listened to their story with growing excitement.

"So that horse does carry the Chandler brand, eh?" he replied. "I thought it was strange a wild horse would come up so close to ranch buildings. That explains it."

"It still doesn't explain how he got out in the hills

in the first place," Aunt Abigail said. "Like I told you, we saw his grave, and the insurance adjuster had the horse dug up so he could look at the body to be sure he was dead. I can't understand what happened."

"Neither can I." Pete picked up his hat and jammed it on his head. "But I'm not goin' to sit here wonderin' about it right now. I can do my wondering about it after the boys and I go out there and get him."

The foreman and his men rode out to the place where the horse was tied in his corral. They gave him water and hay and bunked down in the dilapidated cabin until morning before trying to do anything with Nugget.

Even though there were five of them – the most experienced horsemen on the ranch – they did not find it easy to get the stallion out of the corral and move him back to the ranch. Taking off the hobbles consumed three hours. Once the big horse started moving, they had to watch him every moment lest he bite or kick or strike one of them with his front hooves.

When they finally got him to the ranch and in a box stall in the barn, Aunt Abigail insisted on going out in her wheelchair to see him.

"That's Nugget," she said. "I'd have recognized him anywhere."

At the sound of her voice, the big horse's ears straightened and he seemed to cock his head to one side.

"Nugget," she said softly. "Nugget."

There was response there. The big horse still didn't remember her completely, but back in the far reaches of his mind was a dim recollection of sounds like that. Sounds that meant kindness and warmth and relief from suffering.

"Nugget." She raised her voice.

He did not make any other move of recognition, but the time would come when that gentle voice and kindness would quiet his savage heart and make him as gentle as one of the horses reserved for older guests.

"I've got an errand to run tomorrow, Twyla," Aunt Abigail said when they went back to the house once more. "Would you drive me to town?"

"Of course." But she wasn't thinking of her aunt or the trip they would be making the following morning. She was thinking of John and the way he had deceived her.

"I've got to go to town and notify the insurance company about Nugget," she said. "We had him covered with insurance, you know, and they paid off when we thought he was killed. I'll have to pay them back."

"Why are you getting in touch with them?" Twyla asked. "And why would you think about paying them back? You put in the claim in good faith. You thought the horse was dead when you did it."

"But he wasn't."

"They don't know that. It's been so long ago they've

probably forgotten all about it," Twyla went on. "If you don't say anything, they probably wouldn't even remember it."

Aunt Abigail's gaze met hers. "But I do," she said simply. "And God does."

A strange look gleamed in the girl's eyes. "You mean you–you'd let your religion interfere in a thing like this?" she asked incredulously.

"I wouldn't let it interfere," her aunt told her. "But as a Christian, I have to let my faith guide my life."

Twyla laughed mockingly. "I've never heard of anything so ridiculous," she said. Nevertheless, she was unusually quiet for the rest of the evening.

When Felicia and Joan came back to their room that night to go to bed, Twyla was sitting in the dark, staring out the window.

"Oh, there you are," Joan said. "We missed you at dinner."

"I–I wasn't hungry."

"You should have been there. What a meal! The biggest, juiciest steaks you ever saw!"

"I didn't feel like eating."

Felicia went over to her. "We're terribly sorry about John," she said, her voice soft and understanding.

"That's all right." Twyla smiled crookedly. "I should have known he wasn't interested in me. I think in my heart I knew that he was only nice to me because he thought I might influence Aunt Abigail for him."

Felicia sat down across from her. "But that's not what I've been thinking about," Twyla went on.

"Oh."

Twyla looked up. "Do you know what Aunt Abigail's going to do tomorrow morning?" she asked.

Felicia nodded. "I was there when she asked you to take her to town," she said.

But Twyla went on as though she had not even heard what Felicia had said. "She's going in and notify the insurance company that Nugget is still alive. She'll probably have to borrow the money to pay back what they paid her."

"It's the only thing she can do."

Twyla looked up questioningly. "That's what she says, but I don't get it. Why does she have to look after the interests of the insurance company? Why can't she wait, at least, until they find out about it and get in touch with her?"

"The Bible tells us that as Christians we have to let Him have full control of our lives," Felicia explained. "And as Christians, we're supposed to be honest, even in a matter like this, that might cost us a great deal of money."

Twyla was clasping and relaxing her hands nervously. "I've never known a person to do anything like this before," she said. "I always thought Aunt Abigail was no different than I was, but I found out differently. Her faith really means something."

"That's right," Joan said. "She doesn't only talk her faith. She lives it."

Twyla breathed deeply. "I–I don't think I'm so bad," she said quietly. "I try to live the best I can and to help everyone I can. I've never felt that I was so bad I wouldn't go to heaven."

"I used to think the same thing," Felicia told her. "I had the idea that I could do enough good works to go to heaven, but the Bible tells us that we can't do that. It says that we can't work hard enough to be saved, and we can't live a good enough life to be saved." She quoted a Bible verse to prove what she said.

Hurt came to Twyla's eyes. "Then how can a person become good enough to go to heaven?" she asked.

Felicia paused for a moment before continuing.

"The Bible says that God sent His Son to die on the cross for us, so we can be saved by putting our trust in Him."

She went on to outline the way of salvation carefully, step by step. Twyla listened intently. Concern gleamed in her eyes.

At last, she broke in. "If I–I didn't know what Aunt Abigail is going to do regarding the insurance on that horse, I–I could make myself believe that she's no different than I am, but now I–I know differently."

"Would you like to be saved?" Felicia asked her.

She nodded solemnly.

Felicia and Joan went back once more, to be sure she understood completely, and explained how sin came into the world, and with sin, death. They went on to explain how Christ came into the world, lived a sinless life, and died on the cross so she could go to heaven simply by confessing her sinfulness and putting her trust in Him. Only then did they kneel with her to pray.

* * *

On Saturday morning, the sheriff drove out to the ranch to talk with Abigail Chandler and her foreman.

"We got the men who tried to steal your horse," he said. "They were picked up in Denver. I just got back with them last night."

"I'm curious," Abigail said. "Did you find out anything about how Nugget came to be alive when we had been told he was dead?"

The officer nodded. "We certainly did. Do you remember a Charlie Nelson who used to work for you?"

"He's the one who was driving the truck when the trailer came loose and Nugget was supposed to have been killed."

"That's right." The sheriff smiled. "When you asked him to take the stallion over to another ranch in the trailer, he saw a way to get the horse for his own – or thought he did. He got another black horse, put him in the trailer, and contrived to have it go over the cliff, killing the horse. Then he was going to have Nugget for himself."

"But the horse was in the mountains," Aunt Abigail said. "Charlie didn't have him."

"That's just it. The stallion broke away from him and went up into the hills. He'd been hunting for him off and on ever since, but he hadn't been able to find him until the fires drove him out of the high country."

"What about John?" Twyla broke in quickly.

"Well, I feel sorry for that young man. When he came out here, he came at the urging of his employer who wanted to buy Nugget. I don't know how he found out you owned him, Abigail, but he did. So he sent young Sherman out to buy the horse. The young man thought you were giving him the runaround, Abigail, so he started inquiring around, and somebody told Charlie Nelson that he wanted to get his hands on Nugget and was willing to pay a handsome price."

The sheriff paused thoughtfully.

"I guess you know the rest without my telling you. Charlie convinced him that the horse was running wild, and you didn't know anything about it and had no claim on him. When they caught the horse, he leveled with Sherman and convinced the boy he should break into your office and get the papers. The rest of the story you know."

"What do you think they'll do to him?" Twyla asked hesitantly. "Will he be sent to prison?"

"That's up to a judge, of course," he replied, "but I rather imagine he'll get a couple of years."

Tears came to Mrs. Chandler's eyes. "That's too bad."

"I don't think you should feel that way," the sheriff said irritably. "After all, he broke the law. He should pay the penalty."

"That isn't what I'm talking about," she replied. "I was thinking about the times I talked with that young man about trusting Christ as his Savior and he wouldn't listen. If he had, his life might have been different." She looked up at Twyla.

Her niece nodded. "I know." There was something strange in her tone, something that caused Abigail's head to snap erect.

"Yes?" she said questioningly.

Twyla was suddenly flustered. "Didn't Felicia or Joan tell you?"

"We thought it better if you did," Felicia said. "After all, it does concern you."

By this time, everyone else was quiet, looking at Twyla. For a moment, she hesitated. Then a faint smile played across her mouth.

"You won't have to pray for me anymore, Aunt Abigail," she said, "that I commit my life to Christ, I mean. I already have taken care of that."

At first, Mrs. Chandler couldn't believe what she was hearing.

"It was your decision to notify the insurance

company about Nugget and pay them the money they had given you when everyone thought he had been killed," the girl went on. "Up until then, I thought all of this talk about religion was just so much talk and didn't really mean anything. But when you did what you did, I saw that there is something to it after all."

Her smile was sweeter than it had ever been before. "So I confessed my sin and accepted Christ as my Savior."

This time, tears not only came to Aunt Abigail's eyes, they trickled down her cheeks.

"Praise the Lord," she breathed.

Felicia and Joan beamed.

THE
FELICIA CARTRIGHT SERIES

Felicia Cartright, a petite blonde who is one of the most popular students at Wellington School for Girls, has a surprising inclination toward mysteries. If a mysterious situation arises, it either makes its way to Felicia, or Felicia somehow finds it. Though this is a bit trying for her happy-go-lucky roommate, Joan Bailey, it does prevent life from becoming monotonous. It also enables Bernard Palmer, the popular author of the "Danny Orlis" books, to write an entertaining series of stories for girls aged twelve to eighteen.

The mysteries range from a valuable missing antique to an attempt by claim jumpers to steal a deposit of tungsten ore. There's excitement and action galore—but there's also spiritual guidance and blessing because Felicia and her partner-in-adventure love the Lord and take Him into account in all their experiences.

AVAILABLE FROM WWW.ANEKOPRESS.COM

www.ingramcontent.com/pod-product-compliance
Lightning Source LLC
Chambersburg PA
CBHW071519120626
46550CB00006B/2284